WITHDRAWN
BY
WILLIAMSBURG REGIONAL LIBRARY

THE KING
NEW ORLEANS

D0813482

THE **KING** of NEW ORLEANS

GREG KLEIN

WILLIAMSBURG REGIONAL LIBRARY
7770 CROAKER ROAD
WILLIAMSBURG, VIRGINIA 23188

JUL - - 2012

ECW PRESS

Copyright © Greg Klein, 2012

Published by ECW Press
2120 Queen Street East, Suite 200, Toronto, Ontario, Canada M4E 1E2
416-694-3348 / info@ecwpress.com

All rights reserved. No part of this publication may be reproduced, stored in a retrieval system, or transmitted in any form by any process — electronic, mechanical, photocopying, recording, or otherwise — without the prior written permission of the copyright owners and ECW Press. The scanning, uploading, and distribution of this book via the Internet or via any other means without the permission of the publisher is illegal and punishable by law. Please purchase only authorized electronic editions, and do not participate in or encourage electronic piracy of copyrighted materials. Your support of the author's rights is appreciated.

LIBRARY AND ARCHIVES CANADA CATALOGUING IN PUBLICATION

Klein, Greg, 1970-
King of New Orleans : how the Junkyard Dog became
wrestling's first black superstar / Greg Klein.

ISBN 978-1-77041-030-5
ALSO ISSUED AS: 978-1-77090-223-7 (PDF); 978-1-77090-224-4 (EPUB)

1. Ritter, Sylvester, 1952-1998. 2. African American
wrestlers—Louisiana—New Orleans—Biography. 3. Wrestlers—
Louisiana—New Orleans—Biography. 4. Wrestling—United
States. I. Title.

GV1196.R58K54 2012   796.812092   C2011-906980-6

Editor for the press: Michael Holmes
Interior photo credits: Bob Leonard: pages 11, 34, 41, 160; Fred Whitted, Black Heritage Review/R2K: headshot, 22; Fayetteville State University Library Archives: team and captains portraits, 22; George Napolitano: 50, 74, 87, 137, 140, 153, 179; wrealano@aol.com: 105.
Cover and text design: David Gee
Cover photo: George Napolitano
Printing: Webcom   1   2   3   4   5

PRINTED AND BOUND IN CANADA

CONTENTS

A MAN
OF THE PEOPLE

When the Junkyard Dog appeared on the Mid South Wrestling scene, Tanya Dauphine was a ten-year-old living in the projects of St. Bernard Parish, just southeast of New Orleans. Everyone in her family watched wrestling, and she is what you would call a casual fan. She doesn't remember specific matches, and can't name any of the other wrestlers from that era without prompting, but she remembers one thing. When the kids would go out back after the show and play wrestling, she would only be one wrestler. "I was the Junkyard Dog," said the round, middle-aged, dark-skinned woman with the spiderweb tattoo on her chest. "That was my name. I always had to be the Junkyard Dog."

Dauphine wasn't alone in emulating JYD, and her reasons weren't at all unique. "It was the way he used to wrestle," she explained. "He won all his matches."

Dauphine was one of many people I talked to while looking for JYD fans on the streets of New Orleans. I started my search by using the Internet and posting classified ads, but neither had worked. For whatever reason, Craigslist was a bomb, and even the wrestling and social-media web sites weren't helping me connect with fans. So, I decided to take to the streets. It was either an attempt at old-school, shoe-leather reporting or, appropriately, like a JYD-style wrestling vignette. I headed to the Central Business District (CBD) to see if I could find fans of JYD simply by asking people about him. It didn't take long. The CBD is what other cities might call a downtown. It is adjacent to the French Quarter, and is a hub of legal and commercial activity. I walked around for several hours, finding fans at every turn.

"This city loved him," says Gregory Bradley. "Wrestling here went down without him." A native of rural Bogalusa, Louisiana, Bradley now works at Fredrick's Deli on the famous St. Charles Avenue. I caught him on his smoke break, just as he was finishing up a mini-cigar. When I asked him if he knew who the Junkyard Dog was, he responded "Sylvester Ritter," and lit up a second smoke.

Bradley started watching Mid South Wrestling when he was six, and remembers JYD from his earliest days, even before he returned from Calgary with a push. "I remember when he was a bad wrestler, when he lost like 30 matches in a row. Then all of a sudden he started coming to the ring with that wheelbarrow and teaming with Buck Robley. It was like he never lost again. The fans loved him so much. He turned good, and the rest is history."

Bradley said that feuds with Ernie Ladd and the Freebirds stuck out most in his mind. When I asked him about the Butch Reed era and the heated rhetoric Reed used, he was straightforward, "That was just two brothers hating on each other. It happens a lot. That's all I saw with that." Another feud had a bigger effect on him. "Ted DiBiase, now that's the one that broke my heart. I mean, your best friend, the best man at your wedding. How do you go and turn on him like that?"

Actor and producer Clyde R. Jones had a different take on the Reed feud. "You know, everybody knows if two black people use the N-word with one another we don't take it personally. But there is still a line. Butch Reed crossed the line. I think that was the point. They wanted people at home to take notice, to say, 'Wow, he really stepped over the line there.' It became personal, and I think the point was to make it personal to the fans, too. Like, 'he really cut into my skin there.'"

Roger Dickerson remembers JYD's feud with Ernie Ladd for its intensity. "Ernie Ladd, that was the one," he said. "I don't know what it was, but those two couldn't get along for nothing." Dickerson grew up in the Jefferson Parish suburb of Avondale, and now runs his own business, Unlimited Concrete and Restorations. He remembers going to many matches at the Downtown Municipal Auditorium as a kid with his uncle. "It was fun. It was just a thrill to be there. I remember one time I actually met Junkyard Dog. He shook my hand. I was never the same after that."

Despite rumors to the contrary, no one I talked to described the Auditorium as dangerous, even though it may have been in a bad part of town and the crowd could be aggressive. "Some of the fans were violent toward the wrestlers," said B.J. LeBlanc of Marrero, Louisiana. "I remember seeing wrestlers burned with cigarettes, fans pulling knives. And back in the day, if you told somebody wrestling was fake, you'd better be ready to fight."

Still, LeBlanc and the others who attended the matches remember the Auditorium as a good place to watch wrestling. "I used to go with my brother-in-law and we would take a co-worker of his who was black so no one would bother us," said LeBlanc. "But nobody did bother us, anyway. Even back then, everybody went to the matches."

LeBlanc's interest in wrestling predates Mid South and even Tri-State, and goes back to outlaw groups that used to run matches at a gym on Jefferson Parish's west bank. He went to matches at the Auditorium, the Superdome, and the Lakefront Arena. He admits that he preferred going to the modern Lakefront Arena, but he liked watching matches at the Auditorium, as well. "The Superdome wasn't so great," he said. "It was harder to see the matches. I guess it was more the thrill of being there and seeing the big matches."

Unlike the rest of the fans I interviewed, LeBlanc had other favorites besides Junkyard Dog: his all-time top act was the Rock 'n' Roll Express. Still, he cheered for all the good guys, and was a big fan of the Dog. "Junkyard Dog was everybody's favorite. Everybody loved him. It was just the right mix, right personality, right guy. No one even saw the color of his skin."

Jones seconded that assessment. "He wasn't successful because he was a black man. You didn't even see black, you just saw JYD."

Jones's statement echoed in my head. It was the same sentiment that Sylvester Ritter's junior high football coach expressed to me the previous summer.

With JYD, promoter Bill Watts and company had experimented with making a black man the unquestioned star of the show. Some viewed it as a bold move, but most just recognized it for what it was: good business. I hadn't told Jones about Grizzly Smith's prophetic words from 1978, but he nearly nailed them anyway. "I learned a long time ago," Jones said, "green talks. You can have a black guy on the street or some guy who isn't a big star and he may be black to folks. But you take Eddie Murphy — he's not black to people, he's just Eddie Murphy. It was the same way with JYD. He was just a star. You know, Rocky was popular back then, too. He was the ethnic hero, and people loved their ethnic heroes. Junkyard Dog was our Rocky. It may be harder, even in today's multimedia world, for a black man to cross over, but once you do, you can do anything. Junkyard Dog was everybody's hero. Everybody wanted him to win." Added Dickerson, "Whatever it was, it sure worked. I can remember going to the Auditorium and standing in line for hours. People would get there early because it would sell out. They must have sold a lot of tickets."

They did, of course, sell a lot of tickets. By my unscientific estimate, they sold a million in New Orleans alone over a five-year period, almost all thanks to JYD's success. When he left, the era was almost immediately over. For a lot of the New Orleans fans, wrestling has never been the same.

"I still follow it," said LeBlanc. "I'll probably watch it later tonight. But it's different. I liked it more back then. It was more realistic."

When I asked why they liked Junkyard Dog, they all had similar responses. "He won all his matches," said Dickerson. "That's why I liked him. It was just his style. And it never took him very long, either." Many of the people I interviewed, like Bradley, connected with JYD's persona in the ring, "You knew you were in trouble when he started barking and running around. And then the Big Thump, once he put that on you, that was it.

"It used to make me so mad," Bradley continued, "that they could only beat him by cheating."

Of course, if JYD's success had all been in the booking, Watts should have been able to repeat it with Butch Reed or Iceman Parsons or one of the other, more pathetic replacements. Many of these substitutes have been forgotten. When I mentioned their names, more than one fan broke out in laughter.

Hardly a conversation I had ended without dipping into the tragic aspects of Sylvester Ritter's story: the post-WWF years, the drug addiction, the details of his death. More than one person asked, "He's dead now, right?"

"And forgotten," I wanted to add.

Listening to people talk about the Junkyard Dog as real, about his feuds as if they were real, and, of course, about their real emotions when they saw and remembered him, has been an inspiration.

Sylvester Ritter and the character he became, the Junkyard Dog, is in danger of being forgotten in wrestling circles, and in New Orleans. I want to change that. I want us to remember him. I want New Orleans to remember him. I want his fans to remember him.

INTRODUCTION

THIS IS A STORY OF A FAMOUS DOG

from "Atomic Dog," by George Clinton

In 1979, in the Deep South, wrestling promoter "Cowboy" Bill Watts and his top lieutenants, bookers "Big Cat" Ernie Ladd and "Grizzly" Smith, made a decision that can only be called counterintuitive. Well, that's not entirely correct — the rest of the wrestling world, when news of the decision trickled out, most likely called it crazy.

Watts wrestled and played college football at the University of Oklahoma before he became a main-event pro wrestler. He had just taken over part of the wrestling federation formerly known as Tri-State Wrestling from his partner, Leroy McGuirk, a former junior heavyweight world champion. Watts and McGuirk had fundamental differences in business philosophy that were underscored by a 1978 wrestling card at the Louisiana Superdome, a huge New Orleans venue that's home to the National Football League's New Orleans Saints. Watts would dub the event, The Super Show at the Superdome.

The July 22 card was the third that the group had run in its biggest venue in its biggest and soon-to-be best city. The main event was historic, because it featured two black wrestlers. Ladd, the former San Diego Charger and a growing wrestling legend, played the heel, the bad guy. A wrestler named Ray Candy, a massive man with good charisma but little in the way of wrestling ability, played the babyface. With a solid buildup and good promotion, the event drew 23,800 fans and produced $142,675 of gate revenue, both records for the group and outstanding figures for any wrestling promotion at the time. It was obvious to everyone that Tri-State had done an incredible job of drawing black fans to the arena, and those fans erupted with joy when their hero, Candy, beat Ladd.

After the show, McGuirk was asked what he thought about the card. He responded with a racial slur, in effect saying that he disliked seeing a crowd and matches filled with black people. Watts has said that the person who responded was Grizzly Smith, another veteran wrestler turned booker and Watts's longtime lieutenant. Smith told the crusty and, ironically, blind McGuirk that the fans were all a single color. "It's called 'their money's *green*,' and it's the most green we've seen in a long time," Smith said.

In other words, by putting two black wrestlers in the main event, and specifically putting a black wrestler as the lead good guy, the promotion had increased the amount of black fans in the audience, and therefore the amount of money the promoters made.

The lesson was lost on McGuirk, but not on the other businessmen in the room. Watts soon forced a split with his partner, taking the states of Louisiana and Mississippi and keeping the Superdome shows as the crown jewel of the new territory he named Mid South Wrestling. McGuirk took Oklahoma and neighboring Arkansas for his group. Within a few years, he would be out of business.

Watts, on the other hand, would soon be the talk of the wrestling world. Ladd and Smith, who agreed with Watts about the promotion's direction, wound up working for him. However, to give the fans what they wanted, a black superhero — an unbeatable champion of good in a land of racial hatred and violence — they needed a black athlete to be their franchise player.

Watts believed that Candy was not the man for this job. Despite his charisma, he was more of a round, jolly fellow. (He would later weight more than 400 pounds.) Instead, the athletic Watts wanted someone with an athletic background, someone who looked good, who looked like he was a wrestler. He didn't have to look long, or far, for his superhero.

• • •

Sylvester Ritter was born on December 13, 1952, in Wadesboro, North Carolina, not far from Charlotte. A natural athlete, he was good at track and field and wrestling and excellent at football. He played college ball at nearby Fayetteville State and got tryouts with the Houston Oilers and Green Bay Packers, but knee and back injuries put a quick end to his football career. By 1977, he had made his way into professional wrestling. He started wrestling for an outlaw group in the Carolinas, but soon moved to more legitimate territories, with twin tours for the two big Tennessee promoters, Jerry Jarrett and Nick Gulas, in western and eastern parts of the state, respectively.

Ritter ventured into Tri-State territory early in his career. Watts liked his potential, but thought he was a disaster in the ring. Ritter wrestled as a heel jobber during his first run in the territory, losing virtually all of his matches. In contrast to his later career, when JYD would crush foes in a minute or less, most of his early losses were quick squashes, matches where he got in little offense. Watts ended up telling Ritter that he had a place for him if he could go off and learn how to work. "The promoter fired him," Ladd said shortly before his death in a 2006 interview with steelbeltwrestling.com. "That's how bad he was. But he also told him, 'When you learn your skill, your craft, your trade, you come back and we'll use you.' And the rest is history."

The place he learned was Calgary, Alberta, Canada. Getting booked in Canada's most storied territory took an incredible confluence of events. Grizzly Smith's son, known in the business as Jake Roberts, was heading into Canada and suggested Ritter come with him.

Ritter had already met several key members of the Hart family, sons of legendary Calgary promoter Stu Hart. In his first year in the business, Ritter got booked onto some tours in Puerto Rico and Germany. He had met Bret and Smith Hart in Puerto Rico. In Germany, he met Stu's oldest son, Bruce Hart, who handled the booking and office duties for Stampede Wrestling.

Bruce hired Ritter, brought him to Calgary, and gave him his first main-event push in the business. They nicknamed him "Big Daddy" Ritter, and gave him a gimmick that bordered on offensive — he was portrayed as the big, black womanizer. Ladd himself would play that role at various points in his career as a bad guy, but more regularly his success came from simply being a monster heel who could crush smaller (often white) opponents.

The gimmick worked well enough in roughneck Canada. Ritter won his first singles title, the Calgary version of the North American title, and enjoyed his first stint headlining. In fact, the gimmick worked so well that long after Ritter had left Calgary they were still using a variation of it with longtime Calgary heel "Bad News" Allen.

During his run in Calgary, Ritter feuded in the ring with Jake Roberts. By this time, Watts was breaking away from Tri-State and his old partner McGuirk. Roberts planned to join his father, and invited Ritter to return. In light of Calgary's bitterly cold winters, the oddball, end-of-the-world nature of the city's wrestling scene, and his headline run winding down, Ritter agreed. Soon they were Mid South bound.

• • •

New Orleans has had more than its share of racial problems. A port city, it was one of the biggest hubs of the slave trade of the 17th and 18th centuries. It also had its share of Jim Crow-era abuses, including hangings, lynchings, and Ku Klux Klan (KKK) offenses. In the '50s and '60s, there were civil rights marches and protests. When desegregation hit, the city experienced a wave of white flight, first to the suburbs of Jefferson Parish and the west bank of the Mississippi River, and, later, across the vast Lake Pontchartrain to places like Slidell, Mandeville, and Covington.

In 1956, the Louisiana legislature passed a law banning interracial sporting events. The law did not last; however, the backlash to the civil rights era did. In 1965, the year after the landmark Civil Rights Bill passed, the American Football League (AFL) scheduled its All Star Game at Tulane Stadium, the forerunner to the Superdome in terms of its civic importance to New Orleans. Black AFL players found a hostile reception from local business owners, and were denied service at many hotels and restaurants. So, backed by their white teammates, the football players went on strike. They stayed united, and the game ended up being moved to Houston.

In many ways, it was the success of black athletes in football and other sports that convinced Watts that he needed black wrestling stars. Pro wrestling always had a code of protecting the business — a code sometimes called *kayfabe* — and promoters and wrestlers went to great lengths to make sure fans believed the sport was real. Watts, with his own football background, took this effort to greater lengths than most. He went to extremes to stress his wrestlers' athleticism, and he often sought out and groomed men who, like him, had backgrounds in football or amateur wrestling. He also made sure his in-ring and out-of-ring story lines were logical. He took angles that worked in other territories and fine-tuned them until they made sense for his promotion. In fact, one of his biggest angles of all time would need just such a spin.

Because black athletes were excelling in all the other sports, Watts felt that it would expose the business as being fake if no big wrestling stars were black. There had been black wrestling stars up to that point, but none had ever been *the* star in a promotion, and none excited Watts.

He did have some options, however. Ladd himself had been a huge wrestling star since he walked away from pro football stardom a decade earlier. Moreover, Ladd and Watts were great friends and frequent business partners in main events and in Mid South; later they would bond over Christ and Republican politics, as well. However, Ladd was a natural heel. His success came from being a great talker and an imposing figure. He made the perfect foil for a white babyface as the huge, mean black man, but he wasn't cut out to be a black superhero. His knees were giving out, and his run was petering out by the late '70s. His career would end completely in 1984.

Other potential stars were similarly played out. Georgia wrestler "Thunderbolt" Patterson had great charisma as a babyface, but had been around wrestling for decades and no one trusted him enough to base their business on him. Watts and Ladd would use him for special shows, but they felt his personal issues were too much to overcome.

Bobo Brazil was a black wrestler who had been a huge babyface star dating back to the '50s, but he likely wasn't considered. With the exception of Washington D.C., where he was the top star, Brazil almost always wrestled in semi-main events, rather than main events, and,

— like many ethnic babyfaces geared toward bringing in specific audiences — he rarely lost matches, due to the fear of riots.

Watts would also use Mr. USA, Tony Atlas, a favorite of the Atlanta promotion, who was ahead of the curve in terms of steroid-era muscle men. But what Atlas had in mass he lacked in charisma, in-ring skills, and interview technique. Another option, Rocky Johnson, a.k.a. the Soulman, and father of wrestler-turned-movie-star "The Rock" Dwayne Johnson, had more charisma and better interview skills, but like Ladd and Patterson, had been around forever. Rather than go with an older wrestler, Watts decided to find someone he could groom. He had heard about Ritter's progress from Smith, who had heard about it from his son. They invited Ritter back into Mid South with the idea of grooming him for stardom.

The rest wasn't exactly history, and there were certainly problems along the way. For one thing, New Orleans, the state of Louisiana, and the rest of the territory were still feeling the backlash of the civil rights era. New Orleans, in particular, had become a troubled city in the '70s. Crime was rampant. The police response was to crack down overwhelmingly on the black community, causing resentment and anger. More than 60 percent of the city's population was black, but the police and the politicians were almost all white. Civil rights–style protests and rallies sprang up. In 1977, the city elected its first black mayor, Ernest "Dutch" Morial. New Orleans was ripe for a black wrestler to be its top star; as for the rest of the territory, that question was still open.

• • •

In 1975, the Superdome opened. Home to the Saints, the 'Dome replaced Tulane Stadium and rivaled the smaller Astrodome in Houston as an indoor sports venue.

At the time, the NFL teams only played 14 games a year, so the Saints only had seven regular-season home games. Sensing the 'Dome's need for other events, and the huge money that could be made from running a successful wrestling show, Tri-State's local TV affiliate, WGNO, suggested that McGuirk and Watts run a Superdome show in 1976. In exchange for free advertising, the station and the promotion would split the gate revenue. On July 17, 1976, National Wrestling Alliance World Champion Terry Funk defended his title against Watts, winning when the match was stopped because Watts was bleeding excessively. A local rivalry was featured in the semi-main event, in which Dick Murdoch beat Killer Karl Kox. The show drew 17,000 fans and about $75,000 in gate revenue.

The show's spectacular success didn't immediately spawn a return engagement. New Orleans had been considered a dead city for so many years, decades even, that there was caution about running a show in the city regularly, let alone one in a venue the size of the Superdome. With the high cost associated with the show, and Lord knows how many pay-offs that went along with running in the corrupt, good-old-boy world of Louisiana politics, the promotion decided to wait and run the 'Dome only with loaded-up shows and main events with super-hot buildup.

They didn't return until April 1978. The third Superdome show featured Ladd versus Candy on July 22 of that year. From then on, the Superdome show became a regular event, held three to five times a year, with booking done to lead up to and climax at the 'Dome. Since much of the July '78 crowd came from walkups and same-day sales, and much of that crowd was black, it was clear what the promotion needed. Well, it was clear to everyone but McGuirk.

• • •

Ritter arrived in Mid South in late 1979 looking like a star. At 300 pounds, he was tall, athletic, and probably already enhanced by steroids. He looked like a champion, had charisma, and could do a decent interview. When Watts — one of wrestling's better talkers — got through with him, Ritter could do a great interview. However, what he couldn't really do was work (perform a realistic-looking match), which was ironic, since he had been a decent high school wrestler.

For Watts, this presented a dilemma, as he had based much of his territory's cred on realism. However, he felt he could sell Ritter as an athlete, if not actually program him to be a mighty worker in the ring. Therefore, he decided that Ritter had enough of the qualities he was looking for, and his limitations could be handled.

For a ring name, Watts chose the Junkyard Dog, based on a line from Jim Croce's song "Bad, Bad Leroy Brown" which went, "badder than old King Kong, meaner than a junkyard dog." It wouldn't be a stretch to say that most everyone in the wrestling world expected him to fail. They expected Watts to fail, that is, not the Junkyard Dog; the wrestling world at large mostly had no idea who JYD was. After all, despite Watts's polish as a booker and a main eventer, he was featuring an unknown, inexperienced black wrestler as his leading star in a dead region for wrestling, including a city with little history of supporting the sport.

Even McGuirk, the source of so much conflict with Watts, must have thought he'd put one over on his partner. Oklahoma had always been the heart of Tri-State. When his wrestlers ended up in Louisiana and Mississippi in the old days, it usually meant they were being punished with smaller venues, crowds, and, worst of all, paydays.

Conventional wisdom, as it so often does, proved to be wrong when it came to Watts, JYD, and the new Mid South. At first, JYD came to the ring with a wheelbarrow full of junk, a wrestling version of the television show *Sanford and Son*. That gimmick didn't stick. However, another one did stick: a dog collar around JYD's neck that was attached to a steel chain. In fact, the gimmick would be used for JYD's specialty grudge matches, called Dog Collar matches, and would be with him for the rest of his wrestling career. Music played a big role in JYD's success, too. Before music videos and before most wrestlers had theme songs, Queen's "Another One Bites the Dust" would shake and groove to announce JYD's entrance. Later, he added a song called "Atomic Dog" by George Clinton to the mix, as well.

The music worked. One by one, all of Mid South's villains did indeed bite the dust. To make up for JYD's lack of in-ring skills, his matches were kept short: often he won in two minutes or less. It added to the effect. Not only could he beat every bad guy in town, but he dispatched them in quick fashion, much quicker than the other babyfaces in town usually did. "Junkyard Dog doesn't get paid by the hour," Watts would often say. Quickly, JYD took his spot at the top of the wrestling cards and was winning title belts. Watts met more than a little resistance from the old, white guard who, like McGuirk, disliked all the black faces in the crowd. More than that, however, they hated the idea of a big, superhuman black man taking everything the white villains could throw at him and dispatching them as if they were nothing. Watts defended his star and his business with the utmost seriousness. He was even known to threaten a good old boy or two. Given his history of violent confrontations, Watts undoubtedly would have made good on his threats, if necessary.

In less than a year, Mid South, particularly New Orleans, was on fire. JYD's first appearance at the Superdome came on August 2, 1980. He headlined the show, and attracted the biggest gate and crowd in the 'Dome's history. The show also set the U.S. attendance record for an indoor wrestling event.

The gate shocked the rest of the wrestling world. Two wrestlers no one had heard of, and a promoter most everyone expected to fail, had gone into a dead wrestling city and come up with one of the biggest crowds in history. "Their money's green, and it's more than we've seen in a long time," Smith had said two years earlier. For the next four years, they would see a lot more green with JYD on top.

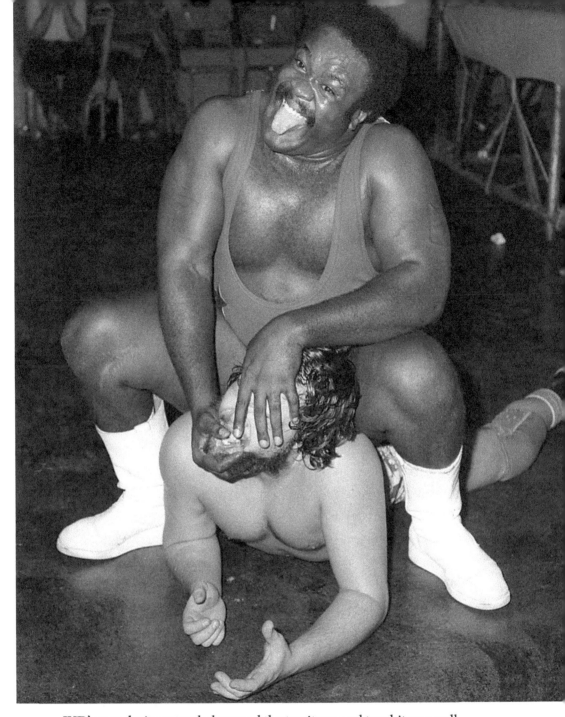

JYD's popularity extended around the territory, and to whites as well as blacks. Watts soon claimed Oklahoma and Arkansas from McGuirk, and worked out a deal with Houston promoter Paul Boesch to extend into Texas. However, nowhere in Mid South, or even in all of America, was a city and a wrestler more on fire than JYD and New Orleans. Through weekly cards at the Downtown Municipal Auditorium, dubbed The Dog's Yard, and the regular Superdome shows, New Orleans likely drew more than one million fans over a four- or five-year period. No other city in America even came close to that figure. Worldwide, probably only Tokyo and Mexico City did better, and they were the two biggest cities on the planet, 20 or 30 times larger than New Orleans, and with multiple wrestling promotions. New Orleans and Mid South fans believed in their hero and ferociously — sometimes violently — hated his opponents. As JYD dispatched heel after heel and worked his way into grudge match after grudge match, a chant began to form that is now part of New Orleans lore for another reason. "Who Dat? Who Dat? Who Dat think they gunna beat that Dog?"

• • •

The origins of the "Who Dat" chant have caused controversy in New Orleans, where fans of the 2010 Super Bowl champion Saints are called the "Who Dat Nation."

Several facts are not in dispute. The phrase dates back to late-19th century minstrel lyrics. Paul Laurence Dunbar, a black poet of some regard, wrote the lyrics to a song called, "Who Dat Say Chicken in Dis Crowd" for a show performed by a troupe led by Edward E. Rice. The saying caught on, and was passed along through other forms of entertainment, particularly in the black community in the South. A popular 20th-century vaudeville routine played it as a riff, asking, "Who dat say who dat?" Harpo Marx even picked up on the phrase and used it in a song called "Gabriel (Who Dat Man?)" in the 1937 movie *A Day at the Races.*

In 1983, a music studio operator heard the chant at a Saints game and recorded a version as part of the chorus to "When the Saints Go

Marching In." The studio owner, Steve Monistere, recruited country music star Aaron Neville to record the song. A local sports anchor, former baseball player Ron Swoboda, got the exclusive rights to air the song on his Monday Night Football pregame show, and the song and the chant became part of Saints lore.

All of this information was noted by the New Orleans *Times-Picayune* in a 2009 front-page article by Dave Walker. The piece ran more than a full page and thousands of words, yet never mentioned the Junkyard Dog. However, even Walker notes the controversy over the origins. Early in the 1983 football season, Swoboda's colleague, high school-sports anchor Ken Berthelot, rode with a local high school team, the Saint Augustine Purple Knights, as they went to a game. The players on the bus chanted, "Who Dat talk about beating St. Aug?" Swoboda heard the chant on some footage Berthelot brought back to the studio. "I thought it was the coolest thing in the world," he said. Soon, he started playing the chant several times a week on his sports reports. At the same time, the chant began to be used for the Saints.

However, the chant predated St. Aug. In the 1979 football state championship, Patterson High School, of Patterson, Louisiana, upset New Orleans powerhouse John Curtis in the Superdome in the 2A Championship. The Patterson fans chanted for their Lumberjacks, "Who dat sat they're going to beat those jacks?" Football chants are bound to be copied and spread around, much as cheers from cheerleaders get heard and picked up by rival squads. However, the chant for the Junkyard Dog may be the missing link that brought the chant to the Saints. JYD's rise to stardom in '79 inspired his own "Who Dat" chant. His fame grew with the 1980 Superdome match, and the chant was ubiquitous for him in New Orleans until his departure from Mid South in 1984. In 1983, both St. Augustine and the Saints started the chant, as well.

It is possible, of course, that Junkyard Dog's "Who Dat" chant didn't directly lead to the Saints' "Who Dat" cheer in the same building.

However, JYD has been erased from the timeline completely, not just by Walker and the *Times-Picayune*.

The Junkyard Dog is a forgotten hero, both in New Orleans, where he was once king, and throughout the Deep South, where his superhero push defied conventional wisdom and perhaps even common sense. His decline in wrestling after leaving Mid South in 1984 and his untimely death in a 1998 car accident have taken him away from us, not just in body, but in spirit, too.

This book aims to correct that mistake. The story returns to a time where race relations in New Orleans and in the South provided fresh scars and deep wounds, often literal ones, to its black population. The story chronicles the promoter and bookers who recognized the legions of black fans who longed for one of their own on top, and responded by giving those fans the first-ever black wrestler to be the absolute star of the show. Most of all, the story looks at the man they chose, Sylvester Ritter, the Junkyard Dog, his tragic life and wonderful, if limited, run as an icon of New Orleans and superhero of the South.

Somewhere deep in the memories of the city and the region, and in the hearts of the wrestling fans that came of age in the late '70s and early '80s, the Junkyard Dog lives. This story is for them.

CHAPTER ONE

SYLVESTER RITTER

Anson County, North Carolina, was first settled in the colonial era. Although its roots are in the wilderness, its long history has mostly been agricultural, a boom-and-bust growth cycle that went bust in the '90s, when most of the local textile mills closed down. Its county seat had a similar fate; the first one, on the Pee Dee River, was prone to flooding. A second attempt, called Newtown, was located away from the river, and was renamed Wadesboro in 1787 in honor of local Revolutionary War minuteman Colonel Thomas Wade, who died that year. For three days in 1865, the town played host to part of Sherman's army while it was on its march north. More recently, invaders came from Hollywood: *The Color Purple* was filmed in the county.

Modern Wadesboro has about 5,000 residents, nearly 20 percent of the population of still-rural Anson County. The town is less than an hour east of booming Charlotte, but it has experienced very little of the suburban growth of neighboring Union County. Its eastern neighbor, Rockingham, with its famous NASCAR track, has had more success, but it, too, is suffering these days as the motor sport pulls back from its southern roots and sends its races nationwide.

Wadesboro has seen similar migration, as the cotton business has faded and the few mills that remain have been converted to make synthetic materials. "Today, our chief export is people," says Wadesboro town manager John Witherspoon. "We're exporting our workforce elsewhere."

To say the town was booming in the '50s is probably an exaggeration, but things were different: more Mayberry, less a southern version of the rust belt. Then, as now, the population was fairly evenly split between white and black. But the Wadesboro where Sylvester Ritter grew up had its problems, too. At times, in Wadesboro, as in wrestling, Ritter stood in the middle of the controversy.

He was born on December 13, 1952, to Bertha Lee Ritter and John Wall. Ritter's father was an absentee dad, a pattern Sylvester would largely repeat with his own children. His mother, too, would disappear at times; Sylvester and his sister, Christine, were mostly raised by their grandmother, Arzzie Lee Ritter, alongside their cousins, Vera and Carl Ray Ritter. Sylvester also had a half-brother, Calvin Colson, who grew up elsewhere. Very few of Sylvester's friends and neighbors remember seeing or even hearing about John Wall. Bertha Ritter was gone long enough that her children and the people around them referred to Arzzie as their mother.

In 1965, under a federal order, North Carolina began combining and integrating schools. At the time, the black kids went to Fasion School and the white kids went to Bowman, a short distance away. Bowman's junior-high football coach, Ed Emory, took an interest in some of the athletes at Fasion and began inviting them to play at the larger school. Today, "Coach," as he is still known, is a city councilman in Wadesboro, having returned to Anson County after a long career coaching in the college ranks. He remembers Ritter coming over in the first wave of players: "Tommy Peguese, he was the first one, and I seem to remember Sylvester and a group of about 17 boys following him. The coach at Fasion, he knew they weren't going to be very good there, but if they came and played for us, then all of them had a chance to win games and go to college." Ritter certainly fell into that group. He was huge, even in junior high, and he learned quickly, playing football for the junior-high team and wrestling on the varsity squad, where his size transcended his age and experience. "In the eighth grade, he was as big as he was the last time I saw him," Emory said, "228 pounds and over six feet tall. He became a real good football player."

Success took a little longer in wrestling, and Ritter encountered the first signs of the racism and hostility that accompanied the forced integration. "We were wrestling farther west, in Hope County, a place that had all sorts of issues, not just with blacks and whites, but with a big Indian population," Emory said. "For four to five years, they had a heavyweight who was about 400 pounds. So I sent Sylvester out there against him as an eighth grader. I told him, 'Sylvester, you might be able to muscle him and get a pin, but whatever you do, don't get underneath him, because he'll squash you.' Sure enough, he goes out there the first minute and tries to shoot on him and wham, he's underneath him. Then all of sudden there's this loud scream, and the heavyweight is jumping up screaming, 'that [racial epithet] bit me.' Well, I thought there was going to be a brawl, the crowd all converging on the mat. So I ran out there and shoved Sylvester down with a forearm and knocked him away from the issue. I asked him, 'Sylvester, what do you think you're doing?' He said, 'He was about to smother me.' I said, 'Son, he won't smother you in three seconds.'"

More serious was the development of a local KKK chapter in Anson County that was intent on preserving segregation. The local grand dragon, Roger Carpenter, had two sons at Bowman. Vernon Carpenter, sometimes known as Birddog, was in the same grade and on the same junior-high team as Ritter. Vernon's older brother, Charles "Fireball" Carpenter, scary name and all, played sports, but was not as interested in them as he was in being a tormentor. The presence of black football players, and specifically the idea of white and black players sharing facilities, sent their father and his group into hysterics. The strong emotions threatened to turn into violence.

One day, Carpenter led a group of 50 or so Klansman to Emory's office. "Roger Carpenter said to me, 'These men would like to speak to you.' I told him he was a father of one of my players, he could speak to me. Well, we worked it out so he could bring in a couple of young fellows with him into my office. He said, 'We're worried you're violating my sons' civil rights.' I asked him, 'You think what now?' He told me that his sons' civil rights were being violated with the black and white locker room. I told him, 'This here's football; it's not a democracy. It's a dictatorship and I'm the dictator.'"

Carpenter and his men went away that day, but no one was happy with the incident or the outcome. "My wife, Virginia, thought we were going to get blown up," Emory said. "She said, 'Coach, I'm putting the babies in the car and I'm going back to Greenville. You're going to get blown up and we're not going to be here.' My superintendent thought we were going to be firebombed."

The Wadesboro story found its way into the press through the *Raleigh News Observer*. When *Sports Illustrated* picked up on the local news, it became a national phenomenon. Of course, this only inflamed emotions more, and worried everyone around the situation. Then it got worse, and Ritter was in the middle of it. "Fireball would sneak into our lockers and steal Sylvester's shirt and put it in the white kids' lockers. Sylvester would get angry and would confront the kids, and he was the most intimidating guy for a seventh or eighth grader," said Emory. "So I tried to get in the middle of it, and it came out that it was Fireball. I told him to go home, he was off the team. Well, his daddy came back and charged me, a full head of steam. I just hit him before he could try anything, and then people broke it up after that. He was so angry he pulled Vernon off the team. Every day, poor Vernon would show up to practice and I'd say, 'Vernon, did your dad say you could play?' He'd say no, so I'd make him run around the field all practice. My wife said, 'Coach, you're crazy. I'm loading the [kids into the] van and going back to Greenville.'"

Eventually, the situation became too inflamed even for Emory. He left Wadesboro for an assistant coaching spot at Wake Forest before becoming head coach at his alma mater, East Carolina University. "Fireball" Carpenter didn't have such a bright future. The Klansman's son is currently in the middle of a 40-year term for drug trafficking.

Ritter continued to thrive in athletics, eventually lettering in football, wrestling, and track and field. Even early on, he liked professional wrestling. Richard Johnson grew up with Ritter, and preceded him at Fayetteville State University by a year. "Sylvester, he didn't have a dad. He used to come over to my house and my dad loved wrestling, so we all used to watch it," said Johnson. "We would watch it every Saturday morning." The local group, Jim Crockett Sr.'s Mid Atlantic Wrestling, was enjoying one of its best runs. Johnson said some of their favorites were Johnny Valentine, George Becker, Haystacks Calhoun, and the Great Bolo.

According to Frank Richardson, the head track coach and assistant football coach at Bowman at the time, Ritter was good at everything.

"I don't recall him on the junior varsity," said Richardson, "he went straight from eighth grade to the varsity. Even in ninth and tenth grade, you could tell he was extremely ambitious, extremely competitive." Richardson remembers Ritter being well liked, as well. "He was precocious. What I mean by that is as a child, his size understated his age. But he was very well liked, very congenial. The teachers tended to like him, and he was very respectful of his teachers. He carried himself very well. He was his own ambassador.

"As a junior and senior, he was always in and out of my house," Richardson said. "My kids were younger than him, but I trusted him with my kids. That's a mark of how much I liked him. One day my son, Frank Jr., had to walk to school, and he was having trouble crossing the highway. He was scared of crossing the highway. Well, Sylvester, he must have gotten himself a car his senior year, because all of a sudden here comes Sylvester in this car. He sees Frank Jr. on the side of the road upset, and he pulled over, put him in the car, and gave him a lift to school. That was the kind of guy he was. He had a heart, and he loved kids."

It was a trait that would serve him well in wrestling. Much like his later friends in the business, Ritter's school friends and coaches describe him as witty and funny, and even back then he had a tendency to the pro wrestling tradition of ribbing, or playing practical jokes. However, according to Coach Richardson, Ritter's teasing of other kids backfired at least once. "We were in track season, and he got to jawing with another kid he knew from football," Richardson said. "Sylvester must have really gotten under his skin, because I had to break it up, and I ended up sending the other kid to my office to get them away from one another. Well, this kid took the starter's pistol from my office and came back on the field. He pointed it at Sylvester and fired it right at his chest. Of course it fired a blank, but Sylvester hit the ground like he'd been shot. When he found out he wasn't, it took five or six football players to hold him back. We dragged him to my office to try to calm him down. We never could. The only thing that calmed him down was when we called for his mother to come get him."

The experience didn't dim Ritter's enthusiasm for jokes, or for enjoying himself, but he worked hard as an athlete, too. He was an all-state senior football player and an all-conference wrestler. His grades were so-so, which hurt his potential for big-time football. "He was excellent at football," Emory said. "He was a four-year starter. He certainly could have played at a Division I school if he had not had trouble with his grades."

Instead, Ritter followed his friend Johnson to Fayetteville State University (FSU), a storied black college an hour east in Fayetteville, North Carolina, where he again excelled at football, playing for the FSU Broncos. He started all four years, playing all over the offensive line. His coach, Raymond McDougal, still coaches golf at Fayetteville, and remembers going to recruit Ritter personally. "I made up my mind while coaching that I was only going to recruit quality guys," McDougal said. "That was Sylvester. He did anything that he could to help the team. He played every position short of punting that we asked him to play. In his senior year, he was one of my captains. I tell you what, you don't necessarily pick the captain based on athletic ability. The captain of our golf team now isn't our best golfer. You pick the best guy. You have to pick someone the team is going to respect. That was Sylvester. He came in and did well from the beginning. He was at home here. We didn't have a wrestling program at Fayetteville, but a lot of the players knew him from wrestling. They knew he could take care of himself. It wasn't a big adjustment for him."

Ritter started for the Broncos for four years, and was one of the top players in the National Association of Intercollegiate Athletics (NAIA) every year. In his junior and senior years, he made all-American for the Central Intercollegiate Athletic Association (CIAA). He wasn't drafted into the NFL, contrary to pro wrestling lore, but he did pave the way

ABOVE: *FSU Broncos Tri Captains: Sylvester Ritter, Glen McKoy, Armond Wrenn.*

BELOW: *Dynamite Broncos, Sylvester Ritter (#69), front row.*

for one of only three Broncos to play big-league football in the school's history. Running back James Godwin had the benefit of playing three years behind Ritter. Godwin ranks as one of the all-time FSU greats, and was drafted by the New York Jets in 1976.

Going into his senior year, Ritter had no idea that he wanted to be a professional wrestler. He had his sights set on professional football, instead, although he seemed to be realistic about his skills. In a campus newspaper interview from the summer before his senior year, he mentioned his training, noting that he had been timed at 5.0 seconds in the 40-yard dash — a decent time for a lineman. Ritter named the World Football League and Canadian Football League as pro options, but he eventually aimed higher. The NFL's Houston Oilers sent him an invitation to their training camp in 1975. Pro wrestling legend and even his Wadesboro obituary have stretched the truth into him being drafted, but there is no evidence to support this. There is also no record of him playing for any team, even in preseason. Ritter did try out with Houston in 1975, but was cut because of knee problems. A year later, he had a tryout with the Green Bay Packers, but injury cut that short, too.

His football dreams dashed, Ritter returned home to North Carolina and took a job as a deputy sheriff for Mecklenburg County, in the greater Charlotte area, not far from Wadesboro. The department held an event where officers got involved in a wrestling tournament. Ritter, with his size and amateur skills, surprised everyone with his dominance. A coworker had some experience as a pro wrestling referee, and suggested Ritter give it a try.

"He used to come by the house all the time," said Richard Johnson, who was pursuing a career in teaching in nearby Hickory. "He told me, 'I'm going to Charlotte to become a wrestler.' He said he was working out with the wrestlers, and had gotten Sonny King to train him. He asked me if I wanted to be his manager. I told him I didn't know anything about wrestling. I was trying to be a coach and a teacher. Years later, he came back when he had left Mid South and signed with the WWF. He said he had signed a million-dollar contract. I asked him, 'Do you still need me to be your manager?'" Johnson's father, John Wilson Johnson, who had kindled the boys' love of wrestling, didn't live long enough to see Ritter become a star, a fact Richard laments. "I wish he could have seen Sylvester wrestle. He would have liked that."

Through the highs and lows of his career, Ritter remained Ritter to his friends. Sometimes he had money; at the end he had less, but he never big-timed his way back home. "He'd come by the house, and we'd have all kinds of conversations," Johnson said. "When he was going through his [first] divorce . . . when I had my own troubles . . . he was more like a brother than a friend." At times, Ritter had to defend his chosen profession, much as all wrestlers did in the era of *kayfabe*. "I remember asking him if it was fake," Johnson said. "He pulled out a pouch filled with money and began counting hundred-dollar bills. 'You can tell me to stop counting when it looks fake to you,' he said."

Inside the business, Ritter had a short adjustment period, at least in terms of getting a push as a top wrestler. Sonny King was working for a local promoter named Pedro Martinez, so Ritter got his first matches in his home state. The outlaw promotion was failing in its battle against Crockett Promotions, and Ritter began to branch out. The next year, in Tennessee, Ritter would get his first real push under the ring name Leroy Rochester. He teamed with Gypsy Joe to win his first-ever title. The duo won a tournament on December 25, 1977, for the National Wrestling Alliance (NWA) Mid-America titles. A month later, they lost them to Lanny Poffo and Bobby Eaton.

From Tennessee, Ritter went on several overseas tours, and had a stint as a jobber in Tri-State before getting his break in Calgary. Although he had amateur wrestling ability, there's little indication that he was able to translate that into professional working ability. Ritter's obituary in *Pro Wrestling Observer* mentions that he often said that

Stu Hart didn't smarten him up to the business. Instead, he claims he was in the ring every night busting heads for real. Finally, his manager, John Foley, pulled him aside and began to teach him the ropes of working a match. By most accounts, Ritter didn't know what he was doing in the ring until his stint in Canada. Although he would become a master showman over the years, he never did become a good worker.

The Harts are the stuff of wrestling legend. Much has been written about Stu Hart and the infamous "dungeon" where he tortured prospective wrestlers. Hart is said to have had a special place in his heart, pun intended, for beating up football players and other big muscle heads. While it might follow that Sylvester Ritter got the Stu Hart treatment, there aren't any famous stories about it. Whether it was his charisma, his wit, or his expected big push in Calgary, Ritter seems to have avoided some of the worst that Hart had to offer. Or perhaps he was tortured and simply survived it. Certainly, his amateur wrestling ability was a mark in his favor, but his size and football background should have made him a target. Whatever the case, the stories aren't part of the Hart lore.

Repackaged as "Big Daddy" and given a borderline-racist gimmick as a black man with a taste for white women, Ritter got a huge push in Calgary. On December 1, 1978, he won his first singles belt, beating Alo Leilana for the Calgary Stampede version of the North American title. For much of the next year, Ritter was in the mix at the top of the Calgary circuit, "married" to Jake Roberts. That is to say, he and Roberts were programmed together, first as a tag team and then as rivals when Roberts turned babyface on Ritter. Often, they were mixed in with the Dynamite Kid and Bret Hart, who were also showing great promise in their early careers. According to Bruce Hart, the Calgary crew liked Ritter immediately. They joked about his inexperience, but they saw in him a genuine ability to make money. He also filled a spot. Hart's previous attempt to create a black heel had ended in failure when Kasavubu had walked out on the promotion.

In the spring of 1979, Ritter lost the North American title to Roberts, only to win it back a month later. During this feud, they had what is now billed as the first ladder match. This match is one of the few from the era that is preserved and available for viewing. In fact, it's part of World Wrestling Entertainment's *The Ladder Matches* DVD. The Roberts-Ritter affair is what might be called an old-school ladder match; that is, the type of match that existed prior to the reinvention of the genre by Shawn Michaels, Bret Hart, and Scott Hall, among others, in the '90s. The Calgary ladder match is the only one on the DVD from either the '70s or the '80s. It is also billed as the first ladder match ever, although the claim is almost impossible to prove. Like most ladder matches of the era, it's not a high-spot classic. It may not even hold up for today's viewers, because there are so few big bumps or innovative moves. Instead, the wrestlers tentatively climb the ladder in an attempt to grab the title and win the championship, only to be gingerly and repeatedly pulled back down.

It isn't that the match, in context, would have been a poor draw or a disappointment, but simply that it pales in comparison to the daredevil standard set by modern ladder matches. In any event, Ritter won and retained his title, oddly enough, by ducking a punch from Roberts while Roberts was outside the ring on the apron. After he missed, Roberts sold it as if he had been hit with a foreign object — perhaps that was the intended finish — and fell to the concrete, even though Ritter never touched him. Ritter then climbed the ladder, retrieved the belt, and won the match.

Not long after the encounter, both Roberts and Ritter left for Louisiana. Ritter dropped the North American title to Larry Lane on August 11, 1979, in Edmonton. But both men were on to the greener, and no doubt in late summer, hotter, pastures of the newly formed Mid South Wrestling. For Roberts, despite, or perhaps because of, his father's involvement, the new territory would be just a whistle stop.

He would work there multiple times in his career, but he earned his greatest successes elsewhere.

For Ritter, however, Mid South would be the promised land. Not only was the territory the place where he would make his name in wrestling, it became the region he would call home for the rest of his life.

The Deep South wasn't the first place you would expect a black wrestler to become a superstar, but it had the right demographics to surprise the wrestling world. And it did just that when Sylvester Ritter became the Junkyard Dog, and the Junkyard Dog became a superhero to the people of New Orleans and the region. The only people who weren't surprised were in the front office of Mid South Wrestling. Starting with the owner and continuing through his chief lieutenants, they were unusual characters, even by wrestling standards. They weren't interested in making history, and they certainly weren't interested in fighting civil rights battles, but they did so, nonetheless. Some might call them rebels, or visionaries, or perhaps just good businessmen, but in a wrestling context they were very close to being outlaws. As it turns out, they were exactly the type of men necessary to turn Sylvester Ritter into the Junkyard Dog — and the Junkyard Dog into a legend.

CHAPTER TWO

WATTS
& COMPANY

William F. Watts was born in 1939 in Oklahoma City, and lived most of his life in the state of Oklahoma. He graduated from high school in Putnam City in 1957, and went to Oklahoma University on an athletic scholarship. By then, he had already married his first wife, Pat, and had a child named Biff, but the marriage failed quickly.

Like a lot of professional wrestlers who came from other athletic endeavors, Watts's college accomplishments have been greatly exaggerated over time. He was a good athlete in high school, and after a car accident in 1960, he started lifting weights and bulked up to more than 300 pounds. However, his sports accomplishments at Oklahoma University were few. The Oklahoma football team, under legendary coach Bud Wilkinson, didn't believe in weight lifting. It was a common misconception in sports in that era that lifting weights made you slower, and coaches preferred their athletes to be small and quick. Watts's normal weight prior to the accident had been about 240 pounds; he claimed the football team wanted him to be about 200 pounds. When he came back as an upperclassman all bulked up, they didn't know what to do with him, so he left Oklahoma for pro football. Watts signed a contract with the Houston Oilers in their second year in the AFL, but he didn't make the team.

At Oklahoma, Watts had trouble with the college football system and the discipline the coaches demanded. Anyone who wrestled for him later in Mid South or other groups will no doubt find great irony in that idea — Watts having trouble with an authority figure who demanded discipline. However, as a young man, he certainly fought authority and lacked a certain amount of discipline himself. Although Wilkinson was beloved in Oklahoma for winning national championships, he ran a boot camp–like training program for football, similar to the kind of system Bear Bryant is famously portrayed as employing at Texas A&M in *The Junction Boys*. In his book, *The Cowboy and The Cross*, Watts wrote, "All of these young men were brutalized for a game, and it was endorsed by an institution of higher learning — with the survivors being given icon status instead of the perpetrators being disciplined. Is that sick or what?" Wilkinson also believed that coaches shouldn't fraternize with their players. Watts said he found himself so far removed from his coach that Wilkinson didn't even know when Watts was getting into trouble outside of college.

Almost from the beginning, he did get into a lot of trouble. Later in life, Watts found Christ, and is quite candid about his faults and sins during that era. Simply put, he had an explosive temper — he was a bully who hurt a lot of people, many of whom, perhaps most of whom, did not deserve it. Even the ones who deserved his ire probably did not deserve the vicious beatings he became known for giving out. The reputation as a bully would follow him into wrestling, especially in his life as a promoter, right up until his final days in the sport. Watts is also quite candid about his years of drinking and philandering. He married his first wife when she became pregnant, ruined his second marriage, and hurt his relationships with his children because of his cheating. He is currently married to his fourth wife, Suzanne. When Suzanne asked about his marriage to his second wife, Ene, and why they got divorced after 26 years, he responded, "It was my fault, because I was a whore."

Even in his professional career, Watts had trouble. His stint at the Oilers' training camp may have ended with him being cut anyway, but he also punched an assistant coach while he was there.

With his personal and professional lives in chaos, Watts was helped by the close-knit world of Oklahoma athletes, men who had made the transition into professional wrestling. Jack Brisco, a champion wrestler at rival Oklahoma State, had started his rise to the top of the wrestling business and often told Watts he would do well at it, too. Oklahoma football star Wahoo McDaniel, who also had success in the pro-football ranks, made the transition to the ring, as well. In late 1962, Watts and McDaniel were out drinking one night, and McDaniel pulled out a check and showed it to his friend. "I don't remember how much it was, but it must have been a couple grand," Watts said. "I asked him where he got it, and he said, 'I got it for wrestling.'" The check was so big, Watts assumed it was for a week or even a month of work. McDaniel stunned Watts when he revealed that the check was for just one match. Watts had never been a fan of pro wrestling growing up, because he thought it wasn't real, but when he saw the check, he, too, realized the money was real. McDaniel made some calls, and Watts soon had a tryout for Oklahoma promoter Leroy McGuirk.

McGuirk had been the NWA world junior heavyweight champion, so he promoted a territory full of junior heavyweights. His star was Danny Hodge, who may have been the toughest man in wrestling ever, despite the fact that he was smaller than most wrestlers. At the least, he had a legendary grip, a vise-like lock that no one could break. Hodge was the longtime reigning champion in the division, which McGuirk booked and largely controlled.

Naturally, Watts stuck out in such a promotion. His size eventually helped him get over in Oklahoma, as it did everywhere, but in the beginning, McGuirk simply had no use for him. Instead, McDaniel got Watts booked into Indianapolis. From there, Watts slowly made the rounds. He worked for Dory Funk Sr. in Amarillo; Morris Sigel in Houston; Jules Strongbow in Los Angeles; Ed McLemore in Dallas; and then began appearing back home for McGuirk, as well. With his size, his aggression, and his amateur wrestling skills, he did well everywhere he went, although he continued to have issues outside the ring.

In 1964, Watts got the first of many big breaks in his career when he was called up to New York to work for Vince J. McMahon and his partner at the time, "Toots" Mondt. Besides his first sustained run as a headliner, Watts also renewed acquaintances with Ene, whom he would later marry. Ene had a son named Joel from her first marriage, and she and Watts would have three more kids, Erik, Micah, and Ene. After nearly two years in New York, and having been made a main-event attraction, Watts wrestled for Roy Shire in San Francisco and Verne Gagne in the Midwest. Shire had taken a territory that had been dead and turned it into a hotbed of wrestling. Watts would later do the same thing with Mid South. After a brief period where he left wrestling to work in direct marketing, Watts moved on to Verne Gagne's Midwest territory, the American Wrestling Association. Gagne won an NCAA wrestling title at Minnesota and represented the United States at the Olympics. He used his success to promote himself into a top-flight pro wrestler, as well. When the NWA cartel didn't make him champion, Gagne claimed his own world title and built his territory into a powerhouse. He thrived, at least initially, on personal associations outside of wrestling, networking his way into powerful alliances with the business leaders and television-station managers who could make his promotion successful . . . or cause its demise.

Working for Shire and Gagne helped Watts's transition toward being a promoter. Each was a genius in his own way, each was successful, and each had giant flaws that would end up dooming their promotions in the ensuing decades, Shire in the '70s and Gagne in the '80s. Some of the influence they had on Watts was positive, but many of the things they taught him were negative. The experiences would pay quick dividends. Soon enough, Watts had the opportunity to put his knowledge to good use.

In 1970, McGuirk called Watts back to Oklahoma to help solve the problems in the territory. In a sense, he had lost control of the business, and his bookers and workers were running the show. Egos were taking precedence over business, which was a common problem in wrestling, as evidenced by the decline of the NWA in the '80s, World Championship Wrestling (WCW) in the '90s, and the more recent struggles of Total Nonstop Action Wrestling (TNA). McGuirk didn't totally trust Watts, so he set up a deal where Gagne and Fritz Von Erich, a new Dallas promoter and a national headliner who used a Nazi gimmick, bought into the partnership. As the star of the territory, Danny Hodge got a percentage, as well.

Hodge, Gagne, and Von Erich were largely silent partners, an arrangement common in the NWA cartel. Watts, however, had no intention of being silent. Returning to Oklahoma after six years on top in the best territories was a step down for him. Only owning part of the territory could make up for all the other issues. "I'd been excited about my first experience as a part owner, but Oklahoma was nothing

but problems," he wrote. "The weather was horrible, the trips were horrible, and the office politics were horrible."

McGuirk had lost the sight in one of his eyes early in his life because of a childhood disease. Despite his handicap, he excelled at amateur wrestling, and went to Oklahoma State, then known as Oklahoma A&M, where he won two NCAA wrestling titles. He was also editor of the college newspaper. His transition into professional wrestling had been smooth. He reigned over the junior heavyweight division in the years before Hodge, and held the NWA title on and off for nearly two decades. His career ended tragically when he lost the sight in his other eye in a bar fight; McGuirk was sucker punched while sticking up for another wrestler, took shards of glass in his eye, and lost his vision.

In wrestling, the loss of a second eye was always blamed on a car accident to avoid insinuating that a wrestler could lose a fight. It was one of those stigmas promoters had; Watts himself would fire wrestlers for losing bar fights. McGuirk reacted to the loss of his vision and his wrestling career with what would now be diagnosed as depression. Watts and several other sources describe McGuirk as alcoholic and moody. "I tried to treat him as a father figure," Watts wrote, "but I never knew where I stood with him." In the office, Watts found McGuirk to be the voice of negativity, always tearing down ideas, always pessimistic about the prospects for success.

In a pattern that's typical of an entrenched promotion in decline, there were many cronies, or stooges in wrestling terms, in McGuirk's office whose careers and lifestyles depended on keeping the status quo. They were anti-Watts from the beginning. Watts said he felt like he had to rid the promotion of the rats and backstabbers to get anything accomplished. He would book the wrestlers who were junior heavyweights to beat Hodge. Hodge would then take his fury out on them in a series of rematches, and the stooges would wisely decide that there were better ways to make a living in wrestling. Watts would run others off by burying them, and since it was Watts, a few probably got the point through bullying, as well.

The roster did improve, and Gagne and Von Erich sent in some talent to replace the dead weight. It was during this period that Watts first began pushing Dale Hey, the wrestler who would become so important to him in the '80s, as Buddy Roberts of the Fabulous Freebirds. It was also in this era that Watts moved the television tapings to Shreveport, where they would stay throughout the Mid South era. Originally, Watts did this to get away from a television announcer he disliked named Danny Williams. Watts said he felt Williams tried too hard to make himself the star of the show, something he hated in announcers. Since Williams worked for the Oklahoma City television station that filmed the show, the shift to Shreveport took the tapings out of Williams's domain. It also introduced Boyd Pierce to the mix. Pierce, the flamboyant, corny, "country as hell" Louisiana native, would become a fixture on Mid South Wrestling. He made the wrestlers and the matches the stars of the show, which Watts felt added credibility to the action.

At about the same time Watts took part ownership of Tri-State, he got an interview with the NWA board to be world champion. The reigning champ, Gene Kiniski, had been on top for four years, a length of time that as a touring champion must have felt like dog years; the champ went all over the country, and at times the world, for something like 300 matches a year. Many of these matches were what were called Broadways, or time-limit draws, often 60 or 90 minutes long. Above all, the champ was tasked with making the local heroes look good so the fans would believe a title change was coming and buy tickets to see it. In reality, title changes were rare in that era. A good champ, however, made it look like just the opposite. Not only did he make the fan favorite look like a world-beater, he made him look that way even if he was a clod, or a green boy, or the promoter's son. Once, around 1985, NWA champ Ric Flair was set to defend against Kerry Von Erich, only no one could find Von Erich. When they did find him, he was passed out in a drug-fueled stupor. They woke him, sent him out for the main event while he was still in his stupor, and Flair still made him look like a world-beater. That was the champion's job.

Watts had other ideas, however. He wanted to be put over, or win, in strong fashion, during his initial foray into each territory. That way, when he finally had to sell for the local hero, everyone would know how tough the champion was. He didn't want to do Broadways, at least of the 60- or 90-minute variety. As he would later say about JYD, he wasn't getting paid by the hour. Plus, Watts knew that he didn't have the fortitude to do 60-minute matches night after night.

The NWA interview didn't go well. On top of that, many of the board members felt that, because of his size, Watts wouldn't look beatable next to the often-smaller stars. Watts ended up getting just one vote: McGuirk's. The title went to Dory Funk Jr., and he, too, had a four-year run with the belt.

Watts immersed himself in his duties as owner/wrestler, but life with McGuirk was hard. Even overcoming the wave of cronies wasn't enough. The top guy wasn't going anywhere, and Watts's ideas about business just didn't match with McGuirk's. According to Watts, McGuirk even wanted to do the announcing. How a blind man could announce what he saw in the ring is one of the great mysteries of wrestling. Still, until Watts came along, no one would tell McGuirk that it was a bad idea.

Ultimately, the negativity and the constant infighting got to be too much. In 1972, Florida promoter Eddie Graham, who would become one of Watts's closest friends in wrestling, asked Watts to work the Georgia territory. The NWA had a promotional war raging in Georgia. Graham was a shareholder in the Georgia office, and he told Watts he needed his help. Eager to be out of the battle in his own promotion, Watts jumped at the chance.

Soon enough, he had Georgia on his mind. At first, Graham was just calling in talent to oppose an outlaw group in a squabble over the territory — Georgia co-owner Ray Gunkel had kicked his partners out and formed his own group in 1972 — at least that had been his intention before he had a heart attack during a match and died in a locker room in Savannah. His widow, Ann, continued with the plans to take over the territory. The NWA cartel lined up against her. All of the local talent went with Gunkel except Bob Armstrong. Since Graham promoted Florida, he had extensive contacts and friendships with the ousted promoters. He also worried that if the outlaws succeeded in Georgia, they would expand into his territory next. He was the point man on the war, calling in talent like Watts to run against the opposition cards.

The NWA group technically owned the television contract on WTBS (then just channel 17, not yet the cable outlet), but Ann Gunkel had some pull with Ted Turner. The wrestling business being the wrestling business, there was a lot of talk about what kind of pull she had. In any event, WTBS wound up airing both promotions back to back, out of the same studio — and getting great ratings for both shows. The war moved to the arenas.

Watts came in for a television taping. The card was loaded with NWA stars who were huge in their own territories but unknown in Georgia. He had been booked to beat Armstrong, but when he saw the reaction Armstrong got from the fans, he changed the finish midmatch and told Armstrong to beat him.

Graham had made Jack Brisco into a star, and Brisco had been telling Graham to keep an eye on his fellow Okie. "The guy you need to get down here is Bill Watts," Watts credits Brisco with telling Graham. Graham was convinced by Brisco's sell job, as well as Watts's immediate understanding of the Georgia situation and his in-ring ad lib with Armstrong. Graham flew Watts to Florida to watch his operation, and his opinion of Watts increased. In the end, Graham offered Watts a booking job in Florida — to start immediately after he helped clean up the mess in Georgia. Eager to get away from McGuirk, Watts agreed. As part of the deal, he became a shareholder in Florida, as well. The war lasted a couple of years. Gunkel's charm helped her hang on, but she eventually filed an anti-trust lawsuit and closed down.

By then, Watts had moved into Florida, where he claims he really learned the business. He learned, or improved upon, his ability to make stars. For example, Watts had a hand in turning Dusty Rhodes babyface and into one of the hottest acts in the country. He helped turn Graham's young talent into budding stars, guys like Dick Slater, Paul Orndorff, and Graham's own son, Mike. He learned about booking for venues where the promotion ran every week, as Florida did in Tampa and Watts would one day do in New Orleans. He also expanded into a second circuit to help maximize profits.

Graham preached credibility, from the action to the announcers, a philosphy that Watts would adopt as his own. Graham had been one of the pioneers of the super show, where every match was of main-event caliber, or at least a big blow off to a hot feud, to maximize crowds for special events. Of course, this philosophy would lead to the Superdome Spectaculars.

Florida was a great territory in its day, and an excellent place to learn. The only downside, as was always the case with wrestling, was the toll it took on family life. At first, Watts tried to keep his family home and visit on the weekends. Then he brought them along. But Ene Watts grew tired of Florida, so she headed back to Oklahoma, and her husband was not far behind. In the end, he'd learned the business from Graham, a crusty old high school dropout who would destroy himself with alcohol, debts, and, after his territory fell apart in the '80s wrestling war, suicide. "He always used to ask," Watts wrote, "'You're a college man. Why are you here working for me, a high school dropout?' I always told him, 'I came to get my Ph.D. in wrestling.'"

In 1975, Watts was back in Tri-State, where he set about putting his house in order. He bought out Von Erich and Gagne, insisted on the promotion keeping professional books — McGuirk had run

Tri-State out of his "back pocket" — and began making things right with McGuirk, as well. When Dick Murdoch's star began to rise, Watts learned the hard way about the curse of the booker's ego. Watts was used to being the top star, so he almost cut Murdoch off at the knees. However, unlike Rhodes and many, many other bookers and promoters, Watts looked at the situation with unbiased eyes and instead cut back on his own push. By 1980, he would be semi-retired, with only a few big comebacks. Like most, he probably came back one time too many. However, in 1975 he was riding high on promoting, and by 1976 he would promote his first Superdome show.

The success should have thrilled McGuirk, but it only seemed to make him angrier. After the 1978 Superdome show, headlined by Ernie Ladd versus Ray Candy, when McGuirk uttered his infamous racial slur against his own promotion and the crowd it had drawn, Watts and their lieutenants were shocked. After Grizzly Smith defended the crowd's color by pointing out that their money was green, Watts jumped in with his own defense. "Leroy, this was the biggest gate we've ever drawn," he said. "It puts us on the map as a major promotion." In response, McGuirk only repeated his slurs. Worse, Ladd had actually been in the room listening. He tiptoed out and then re-entered loudly. At that point, McGuirk changed his demeanor and reportedly gave Ladd a warm greeting and a hug, no doubt congratulating him on the big success in New Orleans. Ladd never let on that he had heard the earlier conversation.

Of course, that was Ernie Ladd, a monster of a man who was well versed in turning the other cheek. Unlike most football players who became wrestlers, Ladd had been a legitimate star as a defensive lineman, first at Grambling State for legendary coach Eddie Robinson, and then for the Sid Gillman's San Diego Chargers in the '60s. He played in three AFL title games, winning the championship in 1963. He was a four-time AFL all-star and a three-time media all-pro. Nicknamed

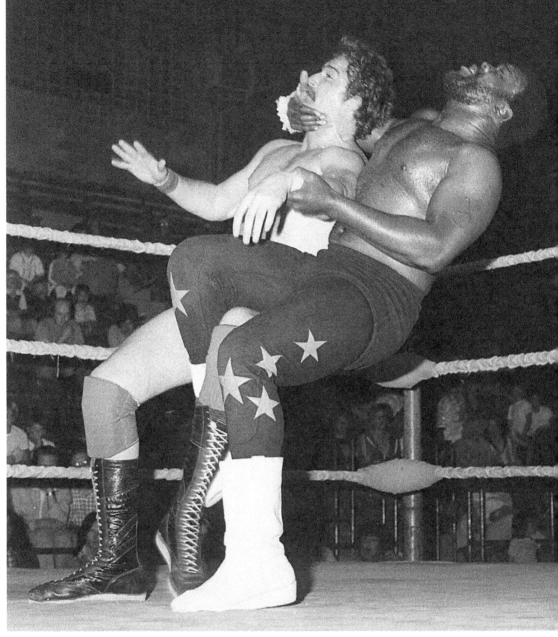

JYD takes Jake "The Snake" Roberts to the mat with a Russian leg sweep.

the Big Cat because of his amazing speed for a man of his size — 6'9"
and more than 300 pounds — he was a giant of his time, an Ed "Too
Tall" Jones of a different era. He played five years for the Chargers,
one for the Oilers, and one for the Chiefs before injuries ended his
career. He spent a couple more seasons on the Chiefs' injured reserve

list, including 1967–68, when the team made the first Superbowl. He was later inducted into the Louisiana Sports Hall of Fame and the San Diego Chargers Hall of Fame.

After his first year of pro football, Ladd began wrestling, at first just in the off-season. He started as part of a publicity stunt in which members of the San Diego wrestling group challenged members of the Chargers. Ladd responded, and showed instant ability. He went to work for the Los Angeles promotion, and his size and interview skills made him an immediate star. Soon, he spent his off-seasons going on the road to various territories. He was a menacing black giant who was good for drawing heat against the smaller white babyfaces who would overcome the odds to battle back and defeat him. Or, in southern promotions, where blacks and whites were often barred from competing against each another, he was the perfect foil for Bobo Brazil, the biggest black star and one of the most popular wrestlers of the era. Ladd made so much money in wrestling that he eventually gave up football altogether.

Brazil is sometimes called the Jackie Robinson of wrestling for his role in the integration of the sport. If that's true, then Ladd was the Larry Doby, the Cleveland Indian who integrated the American League and who is often forgotten in the many tributes to Robinson. Ladd endured as much as his more famous counterpart. Perhaps, because he was the heel in a sport known to induce violent reactions from its fans, Ladd endured even more rage than the crowd-pleasing Brazil. It wasn't just from fans, either. It came from promoters, like McGuirk, and even other wrestlers. Watts remembered one incident that occurred just after Lyndon Johnson signed the landmark Civil Rights Act. In a Baltimore locker room, a journeyman named Don McClarity said to Ladd, with Brazil sitting there, too, "I don't care what the president says," and then proceeded to call Ladd *that* word. Watts thought Ladd was going to kill the smaller wrestler. "But Ernie was thinking so much further ahead than anyone. He was making huge money, and he wasn't going to lose it over a dressing room brawl."

Instead, Ladd focused on the green, working as a main-event wrestler all over the country. Like Watts, he had a great run in the Northeast. With his size and strength, he made a perfect foil for the muscle man Bruno Sammartino. He also had a lengthy run with Andre the Giant. As one of the few wrestlers who could match Andre's size — Andre was billed as 7'5", but in reality he was a tad under seven feet — Ladd was a natural against the Giant. They didn't just fight in the Northeast, they made the circuit, with Ladd following Andre to any booking where there was no natural opponent. Eventually, they would bring the feud to Mid South, as well.

By the mid '70s, Ladd had settled into Tri-State, where he could headline close to his Louisiana home. His friendship with Watts grew during this period, and his mind for wrestling helped him take a role in the office. It was Ladd who shaped the feud with Ray Candy that first lit up the 'Dome. Watts, in fact, resisted the matchup, because he didn't believe in Candy as a headliner. However, he trusted Ladd, and ultimately gave in to the idea. "When he started with us, we put him over like a killer, and he was really getting over with the people," Watts said. "He came to me one day with an idea for him to work with Ray Candy. I said, 'Shit, it won't draw.' He said, 'Trust me, it will draw.' He finally talked me into it. Then he told me his idea was to have Candy beat him on TV to start the thing. I said, '[Ernie] you have got to be nuts. I worked my ass off to get you over here, and Ray Candy's going to beat you?'"

Of course, Ladd's idea paid off with the July 22, 1978, Superdome match, which drew 23,800 fans. Race, however, was still a tough subject, especially in the South, and it was clearly a dividing line, even in the Tri-State office. The Superdome match might not have been the exact point that Watts decided to break away from McGuirk, but it wasn't far from it, either. Watts still didn't believe in Ray Candy in the long term, but both he and Ladd knew they could go a long way with a black star at the top of the promotion. McGuirk certainly wasn't going to go along with that.

In the end, there was more than one issue that led Watts to break away. Many would laugh at the idea of the abrasive Watts being put off by a person as negative as McGuirk, but Watts did, indeed, dislike the constant flow of negativity from his partner. Whether it was the blindness, the alcohol, issues from his childhood, or just the typical bitterness that often developed in a wrestler who was past his prime and losing his grip on the business, McGuirk wasn't a happy person.

Watts has been called many nasty things by his former employees and others in the business. Jake Roberts, who did several tours in Mid South followed by one controversial stint with Watts in WCW, has said that when Watts dies there will be a long line of wrestlers waiting to piss on his grave. That may be true. Watts has been called a screamer, a disciplinarian, a bully even. In WCW, in one of his final stints in wrestling, Watts was a bad fit with the corporate culture of Ted Turner's company; there are legendary stories of him cussing like a sailor, pissing off the office building into the parking lot, and smoking joints on his balcony. It may even be true that McGuirk's bad temper and negativity served as a mirror for Watts, who couldn't stand seeing his own negative traits reflected.

Whatever the case, Watts and McGuirk could no longer coexist. In 1979, Watts was coming into his own as a promoter; he was well trained and had great enthusiasm for his new position in the business and his future plans for the promotion. Finally, he told his partner that he planned to go it alone. McGuirk filed a lawsuit, alleging that Watts had been embezzling funds from the company. However, McGuirk and his wife had kept the books, so it was a hard case to prove. Instead, Watts and McGuirk worked out a deal that let Tri-State keep Oklahoma and

Arkansas, which had been the best parts of the territory. All Watts wanted in return was New Orleans. Of course, the Louisiana State Athletic Commission had a say in that. Chairman Emile Bruneau tried to get the two partners back together to settle their differences, but when McGuirk failed to show up at several planned meetings, Bruneau gave Watts the license to promote shows in Louisiana. With that, Mid South Wrestling was born.

McGuirk's half of the business floundered. He hired George Scott from the Carolinas. Scott earned a good reputation as a booker during a hot period in the '70s, but in some ways he had simply been handed a great formula and great talent. He didn't have a Johnny Valentine in Oklahoma, and he didn't have a history of tag team wars to work with, either. Instead, he had a fading junior heavyweight division, with no stars, in a tough area to travel. He didn't have a stable of wrestlers in Oklahoma City who homesteaded, like in Charlotte — men who also happened to be some of the best workers in the business. Like Watts, he wasn't going to get the biggest stars in wrestling; he was going to have to create stars to keep the business successful. Unlike Watts, however, Scott wasn't able to succeed. In fact, from about 1980 on, George Scott seemed like the type of old-guard booker the business had passed by. Tri-State was just the first of his failures.

Meanwhile, Louisiana was the hot part of the old Tri-State region, thanks to Watts and his team. By 1982, Mid South had bought out McGuirk and controlled Oklahoma and Arkansas, as well. With JYD's success, Watts expanded into Texas, including the huge Houston market, throughout Mississippi, and occasionally back into corners of Kansas and Missouri.

But before he was able to do that, he had to sign or create a black superstar to give his fans what they wanted. The opposition — not from rival promoters, but from society in general — was at times fierce. Inside the business, people assumed Mid South would fail. Instead, it had a historic run on top. In reality, the heyday of New Orleans wrestling only lasted half a decade, from 1979 until 1984. But it was a great time for wrestling — and for New Orleans.

CHAPTER THREE

RACE, RASSLIN', AND NOLA

Before professional wrestling was covered on national cable TV, the ethnic babyface played a big part in the economics of the business. Cities all over the country had their local variations. The Southwest and big cities in Texas and California favored Mexicans. The Crusher was a Midwestern hero, partly because of his Polish heritage. The Northeast specialized in Italians and Puerto Ricans, as evidenced by two World Wide Wrestling Federation (WWWF) babyface champions of the '60s and '70s, Bruno Sammartino and Pedro Morales. Ethnic babyfaces drew big crowds under certain circumstances — a traveling star from Mexico, like Gory Guerrero or Mil Mascaras, could sell out Houston, Los Angeles, or even New York for a big match.

Whatever the reason, these babyfaces often drew the biggest, most passionate crowds. When these favorites lost, especially if it was because of a cheating heel, riots were possible. Ultimately, if they weren't portrayed as invincible, they weren't draws at all. Because of this, ethnic babyfaces were booked to almost never lose. For example, when Morales lost the WWWF belt to Stan Stasiak in Philadelphia, the ring announcer didn't announce the title change with the usual enthusiasm. Instead, when Stasiak won a disputed finish, the referee didn't raise his hand, and the announcer said, "Let's hear it for a great champion, Pedro Morales." Fearing retribution from Morales fans, the WWWF let its audience know that there had been a title change from the safety and distance of the next week's television program. When Sammartino lost the title to the hated "Russian" Ivan Koloff (who was actually from Canada), fears of violence were so high that after Koloff lost the title to Morales, he skipped out on the Northeastern rings for most of the rest of his career, despite the potential for moneymaking rematches.

Of course, ethnic bad guys have also been a staple of wrestling. In the '50s, World War II–inspired German and Japanese villains were in. The cold war added Russians to the mix; the hostage crisis and oil cartels of the '70s created Arab and Iranian heels. Over his career, the Iron Sheik played both Arab and Persian, and during the '90s Gulf War he added Iraqi to his resume. When Sheik Adnan Al-Kassie and Sgt. Slaughter did a pro-Iraqi gimmick in 1991, at the height of the conflict, it was one of the few times that the ethnic card was deemed to be in such bad taste that even the wrestling community rebelled. Still, it didn't hurt Slaughter's career to go from a patriotic, G.I. Joe–sponsored hero to an American turncoat; even though he was nearing retirement and in the worst shape of his career, Slaughter nabbed his only world title run by pretending to be an Iraqi sympathizer.

Pro wrestling critics often base their disapproval on stereotypes and xenophobia in the sport. On one point, at least, critics and supporters agree: wrestling does, in fact, exploit nationality and ethnic stereotypes to create drama. The only difference between the two groups is that wrestling supporters seem to enjoy the use of character. Certainly, they defend it. When Terry Funk's protégé, John "Bradshaw" Layfield, made international headlines for goose stepping during a match on a World Wrestling Entertainment (WWE) tour of Germany, Funk defended him. Writing in his memoirs, *Terry Funk, More than Just Hardcore*, he supports both Bradshaw and the industry practice. "When Bradshaw did his goose stepping, he ended up getting the crap beat out of him in the ring, so it was a case of the heel getting what was coming to him," wrote Funk. "When he sold for Eddy Guerrero and the Undertaker later in the match, he took the idea of what he'd been representing and he destroyed it. Eddy and Undertaker destroyed the whole Nazi regime in that match."

In Mid South, Bill Watts loved ethnic villains as much as any-body. During two periods in the '80s, Watts had Russian headliners. He went so far as to have one of his own "Stampede" comebacks after getting "buried" under a Russian flag. He always seemed to have an undercard Arab character to take a beating, and fellow Okie-turned-Arab Skandar Akbar rotated through the territory as one of the top managers. Kamala played his typical character in Mid South as the Ugandan Giant or, to view it more offensively, a black savage. When Ray Candy returned years later, it was as Kareem Muhammad, a Black Panther/ Muslim–type heel. There were even a few old-school Japanese and Germans along the way — 30 years after their heyday.

Clearly, race played some factor in booking. Kamala, Muhammad, and even Ernie Ladd played on white fears about blacks in general, or black society and culture specifically. However, Watts and bookers of his era were never as blunt as Jim Cornette of Smokey Mountain

Wrestling a decade later. Cornette saw his audience as a bunch of Appalachian rednecks, so he served up a stereotype tag team of black criminals called the Gangstas. As with the Gulf War angle, it was one of the few times the wrestling community showed outrage over an offensive angle based on race or ethnicity. Inside the ring, however, it was just business. Ironically, with little tweaking to the act, a few years later the Gangstas became huge fan favorites in Extreme Championship Wrestling's home base of Philadelphia and the Northeast.

From an outsider's perspective, the South would appear to offer many opportunities to use race-baiting angles like the Gangstas, but even in the South, the demographics vary. The Appalachian areas of Tennessee, Kentucky, and Virginia are almost exclusively white. Pockets of the South, especially the Deep South states along the Gulf Coast, have huge black populations — often more than 30 percent of the total. Louisiana and Mississippi have had two of the largest black populations historically, and continue to do so today. Further, big cities, in the South as well as other places, have always had larger black populations than suburbs. In the Northeast, blacks are most often concentrated in the urban areas, but this is only half true in the Southeast. That is to say, black populations can be quite large in rural areas, too, as in the so-called black belt of western Alabama and in the Mississippi Delta region. However, it is still true that southern cities tend to have even larger black populations. New Orleans itself has at times been more than 70 percent black. Little Rock, Houston, Jackson, and other Mid South cities also had huge black populations. While that makeup has seemingly peaked, and the demographics have changed by a few percentage points in the 21st century, the Mid South era was the height of the peak. In the '80s, blacks made up 70 percent of the population of New Orleans. The states of Louisiana and Mississippi were both close to 35 percent black.

Bill Watts and Ernie Ladd were students of the statistics. When

Ladd was working in opposition to Tri-State in Mississippi and wanted out, he called up Watts and told him he had been studying the populations of Mississippi towns and had decided he couldn't draw enough fans there to make a good living. When they got together and began to work on booking ideas, they both knew enough about the demographics of their region and their biggest city. Ladd's insistence on pushing Ray Candy as the black babyface beating the hated Ernie Ladd didn't just pay off with the one record Superdome crowd. It confirmed for both men that they needed a black babyface to continue to draw big crowds into the future. It was a business decision. Neither man was making a statement for civil rights. To the extent that they were political, they were libertarians; they believed the free market should decide. In some ways, it was just another booking move, except that it was unheard of at the time, and it paid off so well for so long.

Although the Junkyard Dog was the king of New Orleans for the length of his run, it was the decision to base the entire territory around him that really broke barriers. City promotions, as mentioned, often featured an ethnic babyface as the big star. Those stars were mostly Puerto Rican, Italian, or Mexican. However, in a couple of cases they were black.

Sailor Art Thomas had, indeed, been a sailor. He went into the merchant marine academy after leaving the Wisconsin orphanage where he grew up. He got into bodybuilding, and when he left the service he joined a bodybuilding troop. From there it was a short jump into wrestling. By age 19, in 1943, he had become a full-fledged wrestler. He was not only one of the first black stars of the sport, but he was one of the first bodybuilders in wrestling.

He was ahead of his time when it came to muscle-man physiques. In his prime, his size and definition were amazing. By the '60s he was a huge star, headlining in places as diverse as Texas, Washington D.C., and Toronto. In the early '60s, Thomas held the Texas heavyweight title twice, and was the biggest star in Houston, the city-state promotion that would one day join Mid South. Thomas also challenged for the NWA World Title held by Buddy Rogers. He would hold the Detroit version of the world tag team titles with Bobo Brazil, and in the '70s he would claim the World Wrestling Association (WWA) version of the world title in Indianapolis.

As big a star as Thomas was, however, he didn't match the star power of his sometime partner, Bobo Brazil. Born Houston Harris and trained by Joe Savoldi, Brazil was originally called Boo Boo until a typo renamed him Bobo. He was born in 1924, the same year as Thomas, in another future Mid South city, Little Rock, although he ended up making his home in Michigan.

Brazil didn't have the athletic pedigree of Ernie Ladd, or the refined build of Thomas, but he was a huge man at 6'6" and 275 pounds. He got into wrestling in his twenties, and ended up being a headliner for nearly five decades. For many of those years, Brazil was a touring attraction, crisscrossing the country much like an NWA touring champion. In the South, that meant dealing with the issues of Jim Crow and segregation. In many places, there were laws that kept black and white athletes (including wrestlers) from competing against each other. In fact, part of Ladd's success came from the fact that Brazil needed black opponents, and only a huge guy like Ladd, or a monster gimmick like Abdullah the Butcher, could match up with him physically. When cities did allow mixed matches, Brazil was often part of the historic events. For instance, the first integrated match in Atlanta finally took place on October 9, 1970, when Brazil and El Mongol beat Mr. Ito and The Great Ota.

On other occasions, Brazil had urban promotions based around him. During the late '50s and into the '60s, he headlined Washington, D.C. for Capital Sports. Vince McMahon Sr. used Brazil as the top babyface in his home market and as a top star in the rest of his cities.

McMahon also used a black man, James Dudley, as his city promoter, choosing him to run the local Turner Arena. Dudley, who started working for Jess McMahon, Vince Sr.'s father, became the first black to run a major arena. Dudley also managed Brazil at times. In the '70s, Brazil settled down in his home state and worked in the Detroit territory for The Sheik. Brazil held the United States heavyweight title nine times over more than a decade, and was a top star in the territory, arguably the biggest. Certainly he was the top long-term babyface. However, the promoter, the hated Sheik, was really the top star, with everyone else being programmed to try to stop his reign of terror. Later in his career, Brazil was a top star for the Indianapolis promotion, holding its WWA "world" title twice. Although historians don't consider it an actual world title, it was promoted as such, giving Brazil some claim to the mythical title of first black world champion.

Brazil did get programmed into an NWA title feud with Buddy Rogers, challenging Rogers nearly a dozen times across the country during the early '60s. In one match, Brazil defeated Rogers and won the title, but it ended up being a screw job. Brazil returned the title the day after the match, after Rogers claimed he had been injured before the bout. The promotion debunked Rogers's injury claim and billed Brazil as the world champ. However, the NWA did not recognize the title switch; it was likely just a promotional gimmick to avoid having Brazil lose. The local promotion could bill him as the uncrowned champ, and Rogers could continue to be the touring champion.

Regardless, Brazil was a pioneer and a legend in the years before the Junkyard Dog. He also had longevity, headlining for more than 40 years and wrestling into the '90s, retiring only a few years before he died at age 74 in 1998. He was still active in 1979, when Bill Watts went looking for a black superman. In fact, Brazil spent the early '80s headlining for Dick the Bruiser's Indianapolis territory. However, he was 55 years old in 1979, and moving across the country for a seven-day-a-week territory with awful travel conditions could not have been appealing. He also had a popular restaurant named Bobo's Grill in Benton Harbor, Michigan. He worked for the Bruiser out of friendship and a love for the business. Had Watts or Ladd seriously considered Brazil for the spot, he would have likely turned them down and stayed home to run his restaurant and be near his family. Had he accepted, he may well have gotten over and succeeded, but it is doubtful he could have sustained a five-year run on top.

In the '60s, Brazil took a young, black Canadian wrestler named Wayde Bowles under his wing. Bowles was born in Nova Scotia and raised in the wrestling hotbed of Toronto. He had trained in boxing, been a sparring partner of heavyweight champ George Foreman, and got his wrestling training from Peter Maivia. Later, he would marry Maivia's daughter; together they would have a son who would become one of wrestling's biggest stars. In 1964, long before Sylvester Stallone made the name Rocky famous, Bowles took the monicker Rocky Johnson and began wrestling. By the early '70s he was a star, challenging all over the country for the NWA World Title. He never quite reached the level of Ladd or Brazil — he had a stint in the tag team–heavy Mid Atlantic as masked mid-carder Sweet Ebony Diamond that didn't click, for instance — but he was a star in important territories, like St. Louis, Los Angeles, and parts of Canada.

Johnson might have been a good candidate for Mid South, had Mid South been able to afford him. He was 35 years old and in his prime in 1979. He had good charisma, was a better worker than JYD would ever be, and had good fire on the microphone. He had great success in cities with big black audiences, like Brazil's old stomping grounds, Washington, D.C. As with Brazil, however, it was unlikely that he would turn in his cross-country fame to make thousand-mile round trips from Oklahoma to Louisiana and back. In any event, in 1982 Johnson became a headline attraction for the WWF, working as the number two or three babyface in the federation under Bob Backlund and Jimmy Snuka. So, had he worked for Mid South, he would have likely jumped to the WWF long before JYD. As it was, Johnson didn't actually stay in the WWF through the national expansion. He spent 1983 challenging for the Intercontinental title before settling for the tag team titles, beating the Wild Samoans with partner Tony Atlas. By 1984, when he and Atlas lost the belts, Johnson was winding down. He spent a few months putting over the new talent imported for the national run. When he left, he became semi-retired (no one ever seems to totally retire in wrestling) working for his mother-in-law in Hawaii and overseas. He wouldn't really return until his son became a star, first as Rocky Maivia and then as the Rock. Even then, Johnson only came back for a cameo appearance.

Johnson's partner for the WWF tag team belts, Tony Atlas, was another potential candidate. Unlike the others, who might have seemed too big for Mid South, Atlas would actually end up working for Watts in the early '80s, feuding with Jim Duggan and Ted DiBiase during the Rat Pack days. However, timing plays a big role in wrestling; Atlas, whose real name is Anthony White, was in the middle of his first big run in the WWF in 1979, a run that would end up with him defeating Hulk Hogan. Hogan was three years away from his reign as WWF champion, and would lose feuds to Andre the Giant and WWF champ Bob Backlund, but he was seen as a budding superstar. By booking Atlas to beat Hogan, the WWWF showed that they thought Atlas was a budding superstar as well. In fact, at Shea Stadium in August 1980 — a show with a headline match that featured Bruno Sammartino gaining revenge on his turncoat protégé, Larry Zbyzsko — Atlas challenged for the Intercontinental title. His match against Ken Patera was third from the top, and he would win by count-out.

Atlas might have fit the profile for Watts, but the big money of New York was more than Mid South could ever afford. Vince Sr. was still in charge at that point, and he had good relations with Watts and the other regional promoters. He got his pick of talent, and everyone else respected his choices. Even if Watts had wanted Atlas, he wouldn't have been able to get him. And, like Johnson, Atlas left the territories in 1983 for a job in the WWF. Much like his tag team partner, he wasn't really a big part of the WWF expansion. Although he had a couple of stints with the national WWF, they were mostly spent putting over newer acts. As with the Junkyard Dog, Atlas's career got sidetracked by cocaine, and he never fulfilled his early promise.

If talent and potential had been the only criteria, perhaps Watts would have picked his old friend and Georgia legend Claude "Thunderbolt" Patterson for the spot. Patterson had been a huge star in the early '70s, gaining fame during the time of the Georgia promotional war while Watts was helping the NWA group fight the outlaws. However, Patterson ended up angering the alliance by switching sides, and was blackballed from wrestling for many years. Watts liked Patterson personally, but he also felt that Patterson had a chip on his shoulder. In a way, Patterson was the anti–Ernie Ladd. Ladd turned the other cheek to everything, even gross offenses, and made big box office revenue his entire career. Patterson saw injustice and offense in everything, probably even when it didn't exist, and it cost him a good portion of his career. "I wanted Patterson to succeed in Georgia because I was coming to realize that a promotion needed a black star," Watts wrote. "Just look at the demographics — we had so many loyal black fans it just made sense. Thunderbolt had been through a lot though, and sometimes you couldn't count on him to represent your promotional concepts. He was a loose cannon. It got to the point where I couldn't do much with him because I couldn't count on him."

As it turned out, Patterson did return to wrestling during the JYD era, but not in Mid South. Instead, he returned to his old glory in Georgia. He patched things up with the shareholders of the WTBS wrestling show and Ole Anderson, the partner who ran it. Anderson featured Patterson on his Georgia show before and during his battle with Vince McMahon over the WTBS slot. Patterson co-hosted the television show, and was treated like a legend. He worked a select few television matches and more in-house shows, but didn't make a difference in the war. Unlike many Georgia wrestlers, Patterson didn't make the jump to the Crockett promotions when the NWA bought the WTBS spot from McMahon, and disappeared from wrestling in the aftermath.

With most of the established names out of the question, Watts took a risk on Sylvester Ritter. Still, it was a calculated risk, the type made in wrestling all the time. The uncalculated factor was the political risk that was tied to the history of New Orleans, Louisiana, or NOLA as it is locally known. (For the most part, locals don't call it "Nawlins" — only tourists do. Depending on their ethnic or geographic background, most locals pronounce it New Or-lins or New Or-lee-ins.) In some ways, New Orleans is a typical southern city. In others, it is the antithesis, the simmering Sodom, the city many Southern Baptists blame for a vast number of ills. It is the place where tourists come, do stupid things, and then avoid responsibility for their actions, blaming the city instead; Las Vegas with better food and actual, rather than fabricated, culture. It is not quiet, not polite, and, quite often, not safe. It is also not the sick, sinful city others make it out to be.

It is, however, multicultural, multiracial, and threatened by its environment in multiple ways: half of New Orleans is below sea level, and the city lies directly in a hurricane path. It is heavily Catholic, where most of the rest of the South is largely Protestant, especially Baptist, and it may be the only place in America where insulting the French could get you into a fistfight.

New Orleans has a chip on its shoulder from years of neglect by the federal government and corrupt local and state governments. The chip has gotten bigger in the aftermath of Hurricane Katrina and the

2010 Gulf of Mexico oil spill. Yet, despite its faults, NOLA is home to some of the most passionate, most artistic, most wonderful people in the world. They are proud, faithful, happy people. And they were the Junkyard Dog's people.

New Orleans and southern Louisiana are different from the rest of the South, due to the area's religion, its people, and its mix of French and Spanish culture, but it doesn't differ in terms of race. New Orleans did big business during the slave trade, and Louisiana plantations were typical of the antebellum South. One of the biggest slave revolts took place in nearby Laplace, and anti-Reconstruction riots happened in the heart of New Orleans. Segregation was particularly brutal in Louisiana, where white supremacists had virtual free rein to terrorize black people who wanted to vote or take their place in free society. The civil rights era was a struggle for the city and the region. The backlash to integration and school busing has spurred large-scale white flight, and a private-school industry that continues to thrive.

As in many big cities, there is still de facto segregation, especially in housing. In many ways, racial peace has never been completely achieved. Or at least racial tension still simmers beneath the surface of the culture and the society. This racial injustice was displayed to the world when thousands of mostly black citizens were stranded at the Superdome in the wake of Hurricane Katrina while a white governor, a white president, and their white advisors struggled to help them.

Barack Obama picked a painting that depicts a scene from New Orleans to hang outside the Oval Office. *The Problem We All Live With*, by Norman Rockwell, shows federal marshals escorting a small black girl, Ruby Bridges, into a newly integrated New Orleans school in 1960. You don't have to search too hard to find modern bigots who object to the decision to display the painting outside the president's office.

Moreover, in one historian's opinion, Louisiana has consistently covered up or misleadingly recounted its racist past. James W. Loewen chronicles mistakes and outright lies that history classes and historical sites and markers convey. In his book, *Lies Across America, What Historic Sites Get Wrong*, Loewen gives Louisiana a dubious achievement. "Historical markers and monuments in Louisiana supply a condensed tour of what has gone wrong in black-white relations in American history — and how whites have lied about it."

Loewen points out several examples near New Orleans. The historical marker in Laplace doesn't mention the slave revolt, even though the state has sanctioned a marker that does. For some reason, however, this marker was never ordered, and a private investor came up with an alternate sign that reads, "Town of Laplace, named when a railroad stop was established on the Bazile Laplace plantation in 1883." Not to be outdone, in nearby Colfax, where the single largest revolt against Reconstruction — and democracy itself — took place, the historical marker describes the massacre of 150 black men as "the end of the carpetbag misrule in the South," even though it was not the end of Reconstruction in the South, and the elected officials of Louisiana were not carpetbaggers.

Still, the city of New Orleans itself outdid its rural rivals with the White League racist symbol that was put up to mark the overthrow of the city government. That government, under federal jurisdiction, was ironically led by former Confederate General James Longstreet. The marker saluting the revolt against his command is, in Loewen's opinion, "the most overtly racist icon to white supremacy in the United States." Indeed, from Strom Thurmond to David Duke, America's most prominent racist leaders have gathered and rallied at the marker, placed at the heart of the city, where Canal Street meets the Mississippi River. Dubbed Liberty Place, the Orwellian name celebrates the liberty that racist whites had finally seized in 1877 to suppress black voting rights. The White League marker has since been moved, but it has often been a cause of racial provocations. Someday in the near future, you can imagine a Tea Party rally for its restoration.

Is it any wonder, then, that New Orleans suffered, along with the rest of the South, with another 80 years of segregation after the failure of Reconstruction, and an additional 20 years of backlash after the Civil Rights movement? In some ways, very little has been settled in the city's violent, racist, and oppressive history.

And yet, in the '70s, this was the place where Watts and Ladd decided they needed a black star. That Sylvester Ritter stepped up isn't all that surprising, in retrospect. He had already been a headliner in far-flung Calgary — with a gimmick that used his race for heel heat, no less — and he had the size, physique, and athletic background that Watts wanted. The Junkyard Dog did, indeed, attract the black fans that Mid South Wrestling craved. Large numbers of black fans turned up in New Orleans and throughout the territory to see Watts's new star.

However, one of the most amazing things about the success of Mid South and JYD, given the history of the area and the fresh scars of integration, is that he ended up being a crossover star. With the exception of the legitimate sporting events that Watts emulated, there was nowhere in the South in the '70s and '80s that saw such a mix of races — not to mention sexes and ages — than a wrestling crowd. The multicultural crowd in the old television tapings from Shreveport is inspirational. Black children sit next to white children, and all of them cheer for JYD. Often you see old white women sitting next to twenty-something black men, all of them cheering and booing in unison. This isn't the present day, when SEC football unites and divides the South based on uniform colors, like purple and gold or crimson and white, rather than skin color. This was 1980, when most of the people in the audience remembered a time when the races would not have been allowed to sit — or eat or sleep or go to school — with one another. It's an amazing thing, in retrospect, and despite the fact that it was "just rasslin'," it is a history worth remembering and honoring.

It would not have been possible without Watts and his employees, but it was Sylvester Ritter's charisma that made it work. At the time, he was loved by everyone, or at least almost everyone. He united New Orleans, the state of Louisiana, Mississippi, and, later, Oklahoma, Arkansas, and Texas like no athlete or entertainer before him. As evidenced by the failed attempts to recreate the magic with other performers, JYD had a unique popularity that would never again be matched in Mid South.

In 1979, Watts and Ladd got it right with their booking. Despite the hassles and the headaches, they found their star. The next step, of course, was booking him to be a star and putting him into the right feuds. To do that, they needed a foil for JYD. In some ways, who they picked to headline against him was even more shocking to the wrestling world than the decision to make Sylvester Ritter the top dog. And once again, their decision worked out — in a big, big way.

CHAPTER FOUR

AUGUST 2, 1980

Like the Junkyard Dog, the Fabulous Freebirds were unknown nationally until they hit it big in Mid South. In some ways, they were even more unlikely stars than Sylvester Ritter. But like JYD, their success came paired with popular, iconic music that would become synonymous with their act. After their mutual success took them to the height of the wrestling business, they would have a similar fall from grace.

The Freebirds were a two-man team in the beginning. Michael Seitz entered wrestling at the age of 19 in 1977 under the name of Michael Hayes. Tall and skinny, with long, bleached-blond hair and a grating, smoke-and-whiskey voice, Hayes excelled on the microphone. He was the classic wrestling "talker" — a better worker on the mic than in the ring. For that reason, he became the perfect partner for Terry Gordy.

Two years younger than Hayes, Gordy conned his way into wrestling two years earlier, in 1975. According to wrestling legend, he was only 14 years old at the time. Even then, however, he looked like a wrestler. He made up for his baby face with his height, bulk, and long, curly hair. He was also a natural in the ring, a perfect mix of aggression, strength, and enthusiasm. The one ingredient he lacked, interview skills, Hayes possessed in spades. They first met in eastern Tennessee in 1977, where they likely crossed paths with Ritter, as well, and became a formal tag team in Mississippi in 1978.

In 1978, Mississippi experienced a minor promotional war, a small version of the squabbles that fill the history of pro wrestling territories. Tri-State Wrestling, led by Watts and McGuirk, was being sued by its former promoter, George Culkin. Culkin had decided to promote his own shows and pulled away from Tri-State. He mostly had small towns, inexperienced talent, and marginal success. If Louisiana was a dead area for wrestling, Mississippi was like a desert, or perhaps the dead zones of the nearby Gulf of Mexico, with nothing worth promoting short of Jackson. As noted, McGuirk's wrestlers thought they were being punished if they ended up in that part of the territory. When Watts joined the partnership, it usually only went to Jackson, where it was winning big against the outlaw group. Even with the rest of the state basically free of competition, Culkin's promotion failed. He responded with an anti-trust lawsuit.

On its face, the lawsuit had little merit, since the two promotions fought over little more than the state capital. More likely, it was fueled by lawyers' fees and personal animosity between ex-partners. However, under the surface, Watts himself admits to some classic pro wrestling double crosses. For one, Tri-State employed Culkin's nephew, Jack

Curtis, as a road agent who handled arena shows. Plus, at various times in 1978, Culkin employed both Ernie Ladd and Grizzly Smith. Smith even worked as Culkin's booker, a job Watts felt Smith did without success. For a business filled with double crosses and friends becoming enemies and then becoming friends again, some healthy suspicion of the Mississippi war could be justified. Then, when Culkin's promotion began to fail, Tri-State started taking its talent. Ladd came first, in time to set up his historic Superdome show and feud with Ray Candy. Smith also called Tri-State, hoping to jump, too. Watts convinced him to stay in Mississippi, admitting that Smith's poor booking for Culkin was actually helping Tri-State win the war. When Smith pleaded poverty, Watts claims he arranged for Curtis to bring Smith a weekly gift of $400 to help him feed his family, and to keep him working for the opposition. As a postscript to the Mississippi war, when Watts and McGuirk split and Watts demanded Louisiana for his territory, McGuirk agreed only if Watts took Mississippi and the anti-trust lawsuit with it. Watts agreed, worked out a deal with Culkin, and called off the lawyers. As part of the deal, Culkin became the Mississippi promoter for Mid South. He was one of the promoters who objected to a black man being the star of the show. JYD responded by razzing him endlessly in promos, often mentioning how he would head over to Culkin's house after the matches for a dinner of fried chicken and watermelons.

Before the split, and before Culkin's promotion ended, Tri-State tried to poach Terry Gordy. Watts, perhaps seeing himself in the big, naturally tough 300-pounder with fire in his belly, loved Gordy from the beginning. He tried to get him to come in as a singles wrestler. Gordy, still a teenager, refused to work without his buddy Hayes. They came in as a team. The booker at the time, Buck Robley, apparently didn't like them and wanted to trade them to the Florida promotion, but Watts vetoed the move. He liked Gordy too much to give up on him quickly. However, Watts didn't care for Hayes, at least in the ring.

Watts did appreciate Hayes's ability to talk, and especially his skill at making a crowd hate him. He sensed big money in that ability, if only he could limit Hayes in the ring. He tried his best to transition Hayes into being Gordy's manager.

Old-school pro wrestling managers usually served as mouthpieces for wrestlers who weren't great talkers, so the transition could have worked. In addition, lots of promotions made money using the angle of the good guy who has to go through the monster heel to get at his hated, loudmouth sneak of a manager. Unfortunately for Watts — but fortunately for his promotion — Hayes resisted being taken out of the ring. Gordy, of course, backed his friend. Determined to keep them happy, pacify his booker, groom his young talent, and still limit Hayes in the ring, Watts looked for another solution. Enter Buddy Roberts.

Fifteen years older then Hayes, Roberts, whose real name is Dale Hey, had become an experienced hand in wrestling, especially in the tag ranks. Trained by Ivan Koloff and originally billed as Dale Valentine, brother of wrestling legend Johnny Valentine, Hey had gotten a previous big break in the business from Watts after Watts bought into the Tri-State promotion in 1970. Hey had been wrestling for Midwest promoter Verne Gagne as a jobber, a losing wrestler whose job it was to make the stars look good. Sensing talent, Watts brought him into Oklahoma and made him half of the tag team the Hollywood Blonds, with veteran Jerry Brown. In addition, Watts renamed him Buddy Roberts. Pairing a veteran hand with a green boy in a tag team was a long-held tradition. It gave new life to the veteran and some ring and road wisdom to the rookie. It worked for Hey. Watts, in one of the highest compliments you could give a wrestler, said that he believed Roberts was the type of guy you could beat endlessly without harming him at all in the eyes of the fans. Now, he had the opportunity to give back to Hayes and Gordy.

Roberts gelled with the brash southerners in and out of the ring. Hayes provided the lip, Gordy the power, and Roberts the ring generalship. The threesome clicked even better outside the ring, and they soon became known for their hard-partying ways. Along the way, Hayes started calling Roberts Buddy Jack for his love of Jack Daniels whiskey. Their exploits and consumption became legendary, and for Gordy and many of their running mates, eventually deadly.

Although Roberts was Canadian, the threesome became known as southern rebels of the highest, or lowest, order. Their theme song might have been "Wild Eyed Southern Boys" by the band .38 Special had they not come up with something more creative for their team name. Drawing from the hit song "Freebird," from another southern rock band, the wildly popular Lynyrd Skynyrd, the group became known as the "Fabulous Freebirds." As with JYD, music became a big part of the Freebirds' act. Both JYD and the Freebirds used musical intros, and within a few years every wrestling act followed suit. When television exposure forced the payment of royalties, promotions created their own songs. The Freebirds even recorded a track of their own, with Hayes singing, called "Badstreet, USA," named after their alleged hometown. As musicians, they were no Skynyrd. Actually, they got more comparisons to Van Halen — as an act, not as musicians — with Roberts as the workmanlike brother, Gordy as the spectacular Eddie Van Halen, and Hayes as the less technically sound but flashy showman David Lee Roth. Hayes and Roth even resembled each other; both were tall, thin, and blond. After a while, the resemblance became deliberate, for Hayes at least, with the spandex and the long hair and the vamping. Although their music was pure camp, as a wrestling act the Freebirds were rock stars.

In the spring of 1980, Watts's new acts began to get over. Of course, this meant that the new people's hero, the Junkyard Dog, would soon meet the dirty birds. Because Watts stressed the athletic competition of his promotion most of all, any story line between JYD and the Freebirds would be based on wrestling rivalry. To take it a step further, the rivalry would be developed over the mainstay of most wrestling promotions, the wrestling titles. When the feud began, the Freebirds, specifically Hayes and Gordy, held the Mid South tag team titles, having won them from Watts and Robley in Shreveport in November 1979. Watts stepped out of the picture — he would soon retire from the ring for nearly four years at this point — and JYD became Robley's tag team partner.

Step one in Junkyard Dog's push to superhero status came from winning titles. In a six-week period in the spring of 1980, he won every title in the territory, except the biggest singles title, the North American heavyweight championship. For various reasons, Watts saved that conquest for later. Instead, he loaded up his new star with the other titles he promoted. First, on March 14, 1980, in Shreveport, JYD beat Ladd for the Louisiana state championship. In April, he beat Bull Ramos for the Mississippi state championship. Watts and his announcers made special note of the fact that no wrestler had ever held both titles at the same time. To cap it off, and make the feat that much more amazing, Dog and Robley defeated the Freebirds in Monroe, Louisiana, to win the tag team titles. Suddenly, JYD was no longer just the hot young rookie who had blown through the competition like no other wrestler. He was the guy who had won three titles back to back to back. No doubt, the fans took notice. Of course, the Freebirds vowed revenge.

The Freebirds would not have to wait long for their revenge. In May, Gordy won the Louisiana title from JYD in Shreveport. A month later, Gordy and Roberts won the tag team titles back in New Orleans. Both bouts featured major interference; JYD would never lose any other way in Mid South. Of course, he swore revenge, but that would have to wait longer — until a Superdome event.

To get to the 'Dome, Watts wanted a major angle, something that meant even more than winning back a title. He drew from something more primal than championships, something close to life itself: the gift of sight. The blinding of a competitior had been a major wrestling angle before. It was a huge draw in Los Angeles in 1971, when villainous John Tolos blinded Freddie Blassie, setting up huge crowds for Blassie's revenge, including a California record for attendance. Big angles travelled from promotion to promotion by word of mouth, and copycat angles popped up soon after. Watts claims he heard about the idea from his friend Dusty Rhodes, a main-event star from Florida who often flew in for the big Superdome events.

About a month before the scheduled 'Dome show, the feud between the Birds and JYD escalated to the point where they were fighting over . . . hair. The Birds had tried to embarrass JYD by threatening his locks, but JYD got the upper hand and instead cut off some of Hayes's. The Freebirds swore revenge by challenging JYD to a hair-versus-hair match in which the loser would be shaved bald. Normally under such rules, the hair is cut with a razor or scissors. In this case, Watts added a crucial twist. The hair would be removed by a secret concoction dubbed, the Freebird hair-removing cream. JYD won the match, but Gordy and Roberts attacked from outside the ring. By "mistake" they got the hair-removal cream in JYD's eyes, "blinding" him.

For Watts, the hair cream made the angle more logical and added to Mid South's credibility. A promotion that didn't care about the logical conclusions of every angle or the intelligence of its fans would have the bad guys simply act with malice and blind their foes. The good guy would then sit out until he recovered from the injury, while the bad guy continued to wrestle, or sat out a brief suspension. Eventually, the good guy would demand that the suspension be lifted so he could gain revenge. No one ever went to jail for the crime, although a fan or two surely wondered why the police hadn't gotten involved.

To Watts, such a logical flaw meant the death of promotional credibility. Given his promotional philosophy, he could never allow such a transgression. Plus, he wanted to sell the injury as career ending, an accident that may have caused permanent vision loss. Under such a setup, JYD couldn't even beg for the reinstatement of the Freebirds. By making the blinding an accident, or causing enough doubt that the Freebirds could protest that it had been an accident — even as they gloated about it to the enraged fans — Watts could justify not suspending them. This created the eventual payoff.

To sell the injury, Watts paid JYD to stay home. Video segments were filmed where he went to malls and supermarkets, trying to live life as a blind man. When JYD's daughter, LaToya, was born, Watts used the coincidence for increased heat, filming an interview with JYD in which he lamented not being able to see his baby being born. Fans' sympathy was unbelievable, and the animosity toward the Freebirds was toxic.

Even prior to the '70s, there were already doubters who questioned the legitimacy of pro wrestling, and a blinding angle could certainly be met with skepticism. However, Mid South fans believed. As a testament to their belief, when Watts and his announcers sold that JYD's career was over and he'd have to find a new way to support his young family, thousands of dollars were sent to the Mid South offices as donations. The money came in small amounts, a few one-dollar bills in one envelope, a five in another.

Mid South fans weren't just concerned. With no hope of JYD gaining revenge, they wanted to take matters into their own hands, and several tried. At the time, especially in Mid South, angry fans were commonplace. Often, bad guys hid in the trunk of someone else's car when travelling to or leaving an arena, both so their car wouldn't be vandalized or destroyed, and so they wouldn't be mobbed by angry hordes. Many times, wrestlers were attacked or had to fight their way through the crowd to the dressing room after the match. Occasionally someone was stabbed. For the most unruly crowds, in New Orleans, in particular, Mid South employed a large number of security guards to storm the crowd and protect the wrestlers. Troublemakers were not just stopped — often they were taken to a place known simply as the room, where the guards, Watts, and often the wrestler who was attacked would beat them up to send a message that such violence would earn retaliation. Even with the looming spectre of the room and the visibility of the security, the rabid crowd would sometimes cross the line. With the Freebirds' attack on JYD, it must have seemed inevitable that someone would go too far. And, indeed, someone did.

A few weeks before the Superdome show, JYD appeared on television to say his goodbye. The angle was shot in New Orleans, at the Downtown Municipal Auditorium, rather than at the television studio in Shreveport. As Dave Meltzer, dean of wrestling journalists, wrote in his *Wrestling Observer Newsletter*, "Today this would be 'angle alert,' but in those days, people didn't see it coming." The Freebirds showed up, most likely to attack JYD. Instead, a fan jumped into the ring with a gun and pointed it directly at Hayes. "Don't worry, Dog, I'm covering you," he yelled. The Freebirds were frozen. JYD, selling being blind, couldn't even react. It could have gotten ugly. Instead, security stormed the ring and disarmed the fan, who undoubtedly ended up in the room. Hayes would anger hundreds of thousands of fans during his career, and use underhanded tactics in dozens of big matches and angles, but his heat would never be as great as it was in New Orleans that summer. In one interview, he commented, "I've never in my life felt more threatened than in that era."

The promotion continued to give updates on JYD that stressed he would likely never regain his sight. Certainly, he would never wrestle again. JYD, however, did make one last request. He demanded that the promotion give him one opportunity to get his revenge on Hayes. Of course, the match would take place in New Orleans, at the Superdome Spectacular, in front of a record-setting crowd. Hayes, for his part, kept up the villainous interviews, insulting JYD, New Orleans, the fans, the promotion, and anything else that would turn the heat up higher. Since JYD couldn't see, he requested that the match include an added stipulation: it would be a "dog collar match." Both men would wear dog collars around their necks, each attached to a steel chain. That way, even without his vision, JYD could always have Hayes within his grasp. As a semi-main event, Robley and Rhodes would battle Gordy and Roberts in a double "bull rope" match, with two sets of wrestlers, one heel and one babyface, attached to each other by a bull rope made lethal by the addition of a steel cowbell in the middle. The dual stipulations worked together to add a nice bit of professional wrestling cliché: after months of being cowardly, the Freebirds could neither run nor hide.

On August 2, 1980, more than 26,000 paid to see JYD's revenge. The attendance was actually announced as 36,000, but pro wrestling ticket sales were almost always inflated. To paraphrase Meltzer, even though the truth is impressive, why not make it more impressive with a lie? In reality, the announced gate of $183,000 was probably less than what fans actually paid. Simply put, in the corrupt, kick-back-heavy world of Louisiana politics, some money was likely shaved off the top for the political cronies and criminals. Despite the looseness of the figures, it was the largest crowd and gate in the history of both the territory and New Orleans. In fact, it was the largest indoor crowd in the history of pro wrestling at the time, and for a few weeks it was the second largest gate ever, behind only the 1976 Shea Stadium show in New York City that featured Bruno Sammartino versus Stan Hanson and the closed-circuit broadcast of the Muhammad Ali–Antonio Inoki fiasco from Tokyo. August 1980 turned out to be a big month for wrestling crowds. A week after the Superdome show, Sammartino drew about 30,000 fans for his revenge feud against former protégé Larry Zbyzsko at Shea Stadium. Ticket prices were much higher in New York City than they were in New Orleans, so the Shea show made more than a half-million dollars, blowing away the old record and the Mid South show. However, a similar outdoor show in Tampa, headlined by Dusty Rhodes challenging NWA champ Harley Race, couldn't beat the Superdome numbers.

In August 1980, the Junkyard Dog gained his revenge and beat his hated rival, Michael Hayes. Rhodes and Robley set the tone by winning their match, as well. For at least a week after the event, JYD's "last match" toured around the territory, drawing sellouts everywhere. Of course, JYD won those matches, as well. The promotion had its best week ever, and announced itself as a major player in professional wrestling. According to Meltzer, JYD made $12,000 in seven days, which was unheard of for a grappler at the time. The paycheck didn't shock the world, however, because payoffs were still a pretty well-guarded secret then. However, the news of the huge crowd and gate receipts did travel. Many in wrestling had never heard of Sylvester Ritter or Michael Hayes or Terry Gordy. They knew Buddy Roberts only as a mid-card, or job, guy. They certainly did know Bill Watts, but most had expected him to fail miserably in his attempt to buck the established Tri-State territory by going it alone in a wasteland for professional wrestling.

The next month, the Junkyard Dog and a young wrestler named Terry Orndorff, "brother" of the established headliner Paul Orndorff, would regain the Mid South tag team titles from the Freebirds. The Freebirds would soon, as all good vanquished villains should, hightail it out of town. They would turn up in Georgia and parlay their newfound stardom into a run on national cable television. However, their biggest stardom would come a year later, in Dallas, when they set the wrestling world ablaze again, this time in a feud with the Von Erich family.

For the Junkyard Dog, it was mission accomplished. Mid South had created its superstar. Business would ebb and flow over the next four years, but Mid South would grow into one of the top territories, Watts into one of the top promoters, and the Junkyard Dog into the one of the country's hottest babyfaces. In some ways, August 2, 1980, was the zenith of that era, at least in terms of single-card attendance. In many other ways, the story about the Junkyard Dog had only just begun. More good times, and bad, waited ahead.

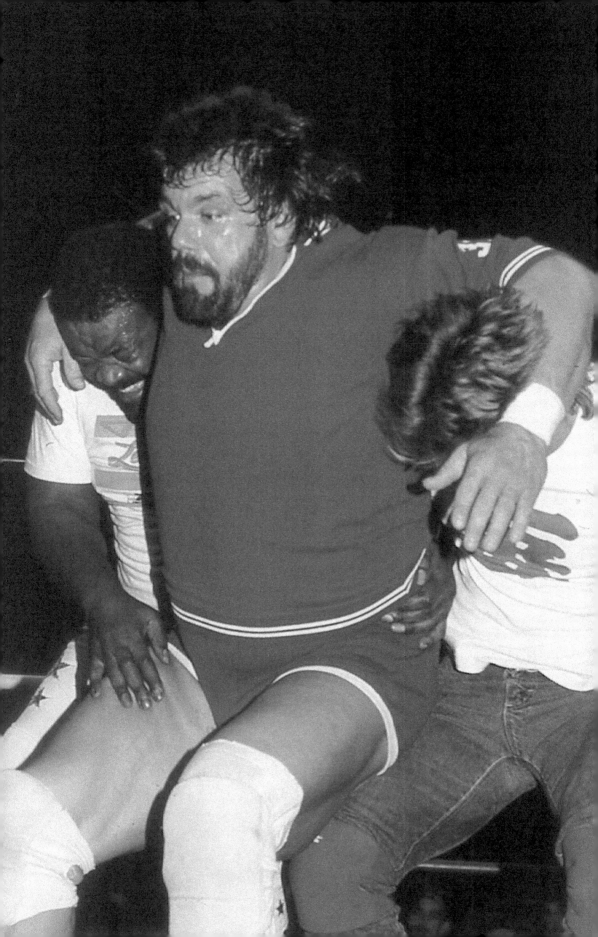

CHAPTER FIVE

A STAR IS BORN

During the 1981–82 academic year, the New Orleans school system took a semi-formal survey of students, asking them which sports star they would most like to meet. When possible, the schools would try to bring that star in to speak to the children, and allow them to meet their hero.

In the early '80s, the New Orleans Saints were a much less successful version of the Minnesota Vikings of the early NFL. The Vikings had made it to four Super Bowl games. Even though they had lost every one, their wild, talented quarterback, Fran Tarkington, became the face of the franchise, and was loved. The Saints wouldn't reach the Super Bowl until 2010. They had hardly ever made the playoffs, either. Mostly, they were bad; sometimes they were awful. The only thing they had going for them was their own beloved quarterback, Archie Manning. Manning is still a city hero, and two of his sons, Peyton and Eli, have gone on to win Super Bowls. When they are not playing against the Saints, the Manning brothers are still the sentimental favorites in New Orleans, because they're Archie's boys.

The local basketball star during that era had a nickname right out of wrestling. "Pistol" Pete Maravich broke or set nearly every basketball record at LSU. He doubled down on local-hero cred when he went to the New Orleans Jazz, the city's NBA franchise at the time.

It would have been natural for New Orleans kids to request a school visit from Manning or Maravich. Instead, most of them voted for someone else: the Junkyard Dog. This would come as a surprise to most of today's New Orleanians; Archie Manning is still an icon, probably more of a hero than in his playing days. Maravich died young, and is regarded as an all-time great — the man who built LSU basketball. It may be hard to believe the Junkyard Dog could rival them in popularity, but it isn't unbelievable to those who were in New Orleans in the early '80s. The reality is, from 1980 to 1984, the Junkyard Dog was *the* biggest star in New Orleans.

There's no proven formula for creating a star, despite what many in wrestling — or other forms of entertainment — believe. Wrestlers who were big in one territory often failed to get over elsewhere. Good booking and a hometown crowd have fooled many wrestlers — and rival promoters — into believing someone is better, or bigger, than they are. Bill Watts knew he had to be careful when he was creating his new headliner, and he tried to tightly control the circumstances of his rise to the top.

"I knew a black would draw blacks," Watts says in *Sex, Lies and*

Headlocks, "but the real secret was not letting a white man save a black man. I put JYD in situations that were fucking impossible and he always saved himself. And guess what? The whites loved him for it. Everyone loved him for it. He was a black man who was his own man."

Of course, he was also a pro wrestler and his every move, angle, and match was scripted or controlled from behind the curtain by an athletic Wizard of Oz. Many times, things went well for JYD, but occasionally they didn't — especially in the early days. At one point, while running a non-televised "house" show, Ernie Ladd booked JYD for a 20-minute match with the Super Destroyer to see what kind of stuff JYD had. Super D, real name Scott Irwin, had good working skills, but he couldn't carry JYD for 20 minutes. JYD blew up — that is, he ran out of breath — quickly. The match was awful. Ladd called Watts afterward and told him his plan wasn't going to fly, because "your guy can't go." According to Watts, he nearly fired Ladd and Irwin that night. Watts told Ladd that he knew JYD's limitations. Their job wasn't to test him; their job was to protect him so his limitations were never visible.

A similar thing happened at an early television taping in Shreveport against the Masked Grappler. Len Denton was from the same mold as a lot of JYD foes. He could work, he could talk, and he should have been the ideal guy to carry JYD to a good match. Apparently, however, he hadn't gotten the memo. As grappling was his gimmick, he took JYD down and kept him down, controlling him on the mat. Even with his high school wrestling background, JYD couldn't break free, and the match looked dismal and one sided. Watts, who would become known for his ability to spin almost anything, couldn't find a way to explain the debacle. The match never aired.

Even the initial characterization of the Junkyard Dog changed. When Ritter arrived from Calgary for his tryout all jacked up and athletic, Watts said he couldn't think of anything but Pat Croche's song, "Bad, Bad Leroy Brown." The song had already been used in wrestling. First, a man named Leroy Rochester took his wrestling name, Leroy Brown, from it. (Coincidentally, Ritter went by the ring name Leroy Rochester in one of his first stops in wrestling, eastern Tennessee.) When Watts heard the song, he focused the line in which Leroy Brown was called "meaner than a junkyard dog." Simple as that, Mid South's hero had a name.

In the beginning, the character clung to the moniker quite literally. JYD rolled a wheelbarrow to the ring and played the role of a real-life junk man. Today, the wheelbarrow would be filled with weapons, and he would use each one on his opponents; that was pretty much New Jack's gimmick in Extreme Championship Wrestling (ECW) ten years later. For the Junkyard Dog and Mid South, however, the initial gimmick didn't stick. Instead, a simple dog collar and chain would become JYD's trademark.

With his gimmick established and his lack of working ability hidden, the character took off in the spring and summer of 1980. The Junkyard Dog's matches were quick affairs designed to make him look like a powerhouse. "JYD doesn't get paid by the hour," Watts said so many times he could have trademarked the phrase. Indeed, almost all of JYD's matches, especially on television, clocked in at less than two minutes. Even when he faced top-flight opponents, JYD beat them quickly. That was part of his success; there would be a group of heels who were on top of the federation, beating the other top babyfaces and causing trouble for the territory. Then JYD would come in and easily beat them all. Even when the heels successfully fought back, most likely by cheating, JYD overcame the odds. As Watts said, no one ever made the save for the Junkyard Dog — JYD always saved himself and any other good guy who needed saving. With this formula, Watts threw a steady rotation of heels to throw at JYD, then they'd leave town to get heat somewhere else. Of course, that was standard procedure for any territory with an established local hero.

Almost immediately, fans fell in love with JYD. "I used to tease him," wrote his friend and running mate Ted DiBiase in his book, *The Million Dollar Man*, "that I would wrestle an hour every night, getting paid peanuts, and he'd walk into the ring, shake his butt to the crowd, howl at the moon, work five minutes, and he was the highest paid guy in the territory. He would just laugh."

The Junkyard Dog's popularity certainly met the expectations of Watts and his bookers. Mid South, and in particular New Orleans, filled arenas with black fans who were overjoyed to see a black star on top. Watts booked JYD very carefully; no one beat him in New Orleans, and his opponents rarely got one over on him. On the few occasions they did, it made for explosive rematches and even bigger crowds. It also made for dangerous nights for the heels who opposed him. "Because of my feud with JYD, I had to be very careful," DiBiase said. "I was getting booed like never before and people literally wanted to kill me." Often, people tried. As mentioned, fans were known to throw rocks, bottles, and batteries, and attack cars as the heels left the arenas. After his heel turn, DiBiase rode with someone else so the fans wouldn't destroy his car. On at least one occasion he rode with Grizzly Smith and someone slashed Smith's tires. In 1984, during the Last Stampede feud, a pre-liminary wrestler, Tony Zane, got stabbed in New Orleans while he was going out for his match. When Jim Cornette heard this news, he tried to back out of his bout, screaming, "They just stabbed one of the job guys, they're going to kill me!"

It wasn't just the fans who were dangerous. Mid South had a reputation for being one of the worst territories for travel, because of the awful Oklahoma weather — ice in the winter, tornadoes all summer — the Gulf Coast hurricane season, and the thousands of miles of two-lane highways. The territory was also large: a weekly trip around the entire territory could mean racking up more than 2,000 miles. It was typical for the wrestlers to have to leave a show around 11 p.m., drive 350 miles to Shreveport, and then wake up the next day and drive another 350 miles to the next night's show. After that, they often drove back to Shreveport to be in position to do it all over again the next day. On weekends, Watts booked two or occasionally three shows a day. Off days were rare, and injuries — which many wrestlers worked through — were common. True to his sense of discipline, Watts wouldn't let wrestlers leave matches when they were done working. Everyone left at the same time — after the main event.

DiBiase estimates that he drove about 60,000 miles a year in Mid South, and that some of the guys, depending on where their home bases were, drove much further. The travel was so hard on family life that wrestlers, or their wives, often cracked. Twice, DiBiase fled for his home base of Georgia, where he could wrestle anywhere and be home the same night. Wrestlers in Mid South spent little time at home unless they set up shop in Shreveport. Guys like DiBiase and Butch Reed, who lived outside the territory altogether, spent no time at home. Reed ended up leaving, even though he was the star of the territory.

The Junkyard Dog's second marriage eventually suffered, too, and in that respect he struggled to have a normal life as much as any of the guys. However, in many ways he clearly had it much better. Where a preliminary guy might make $300 a week and subsist on what the boys called "bologna blowouts," JYD made several thousand dollars a week — and that was just in average times. In the Freebird blow-off, he reportedly made $12,000; during the Last Stampede, he made even more. His weekly average as a main eventer was likely $3,000. His life at this point fell into a routine: he drove from town to town, wrestled, and partied.

Everywhere he went, he was received as a hero. Buddy Landel, who was a preliminary wrestler in Mid South in 1982, lived next door to the Junkyard Dog and drove him around. Landel was moved by people's displays of affection for JYD. And JYD responded: Landel often tells stories of him giving money to people who were having trouble.

White fans loved the Junkyard Dog, but clearly the idea of using a black star was an effective way to draw black fans. In New Orleans, The Dog's Yard, the nickname for the Downtown Municipal Auditorium, was packed with black fans weekly. Other towns had a healthy mix of races, and when Mid South added other young, good-looking baby-faces in 1983, a mix of ages and sexes, as well. Wrestling served as a great melting pot in the South in much the same way sports did. Everyone could come together and cheer for the Junkyard Dog.

But not everyone cheered. From the beginning, Watts had trouble with certain promoters who disliked the idea of a black star drawing black crowds while beating back every challenge the white heels threw at him. Much like Leroy McGuirk, certain old-school elements in the South disliked having that many black fans in the audience. In Mississippi, and in particular in Louisiana, some of the old-line patronage appointees expressed their distaste for the way Watts was promoting his business. Watts's typical response was R-rated at best — and threatening at worst. In Louisiana, the athletic commission had set up a system that only allowed one to be licensed. Watts held the license, but to keep it he had to employ political appointees as his "promoters" in each city. Edwin Edwards, who was the Louisiana governor at the time, set up the commission as he set up all the state's business. His friends got money for little or no work, and in return they kicked some of that money back to Edwards's election fund. In most cases, the promoters didn't do any promoting for Watts. They just took their cut. Watts estimates that it cost him about $300,000 a year in payoffs. Ultimately Edwards went to jail for taking these bribes and it is only recently that he has been released from prison.

In 1980, however, that didn't matter. The only thing that was relevant for Watts and Mid South Wrestling was that they'd found their star. The Junkyard Dog had become one of the top names in all of wrestling. He not only headlined Mid South, but made the rounds to the other territories for special events. He made frequent appearances on Georgia television for the cable powerhouse WTBS, which only increased his star power. In 1984, he even wrestled on the David Von Erich memorial show, where Kerry Von Erich won the NWA World Title from Ric Flair. In the ring, in the locker room, and in town after town, JYD showed his special charisma and his ability to connect with fans. With the help of Watts and Ladd, Smith, Buck Robley, Jim Ross, and the other talent in Mid South, JYD became an icon, and his limitations were eclipsed by his popularity. It wouldn't always be that way. Later, Sylvester Ritter's demons would eclipse his wrestling success.

However, in pro wrestling, the popular babyface is only half of the equation. To really make the matches and, for that matter, to really make the hero, Mid South needed great heels. For Junkyard Dog, the promotion also needed guys who could work, who could run circles around the immobile star, draw out the action and carry him to good matches. They needed to be guys who could make JYD look like a superhero, while still keeping heat on themselves. For the fans, they needed hot angles. The Freebird blinding gimmick worked wonders, but Watts knew he couldn't go to such extremes too often. Instead, he found an even better way to pop his crowds and put JYD in matches where he was constantly looking for revenge.

In wrestling terms, it's called the turn or turning heel. One by one, the best workers in the federation, the biggest stars, at times some of the biggest babyfaces — and for story purposes some of the Junkyard Dog's best friends — turned against him. Almost always, the result was box office success.

CHAPTER SIX

WITH FRIENDS LIKE THESE . . .

In the early days of Mid South Wrestling, Bill Watts used a young Dick Murdoch as his top babyface. A second-generation star, Murdoch was a Texas good old boy with immense talent and an even greater ability to coast, joke, and drink his way through life. When he was on, there were few people better in the ring. When he was angry or uninterested, there were few worse people to have working for you. Murdoch often worked for Tri-State Wrestling after Watts became a partner. In fact, he wrestled in the semi-final match of the 1976 Superdome show that featured Terry Funk defending the NWA World Title against Watts.

Murdoch wrestled and beat "Killer" Karl Kox, a Texan bad old guy who was secretly one of Murdoch's best friends and perhaps the biggest influence on his career. The promotion billed it as a "Jim Bowie death match," under which both wrestlers wore blindfolds and had to fight each other "sightless." It was the blowoff to a long-simmering feud that had been white hot in the territory. As such, many people felt that Murdoch and Kox, rather than the NWA title match, were what drew the 17,000 fans and made the first Superdome show a success.

Murdoch came and went several times over the following three years, but he maintained his headliner status when he moved back into Mid South. When he heard about the plans for the Junkyard Dog, he expressed disappointment about his star being eclipsed, but being Dick Murdoch, he probably said it in a more colorful way. While he wouldn't leave the territory entirely — he returned several times for Superdome shows — his biggest angle would come years later when he turned heel after taking offense that someone else had become more successful than him. In wrestling, life often inspired angles. To Bill Watts, realism made for the best story lines. Murdoch didn't turn heel on the Junkyard Dog specifically, but he certainly could have. From 1980 to 1984, nearly every other successful babyface in Mid South did, in fact, make such a turn on JYD.

The pattern started almost immediately with Buck Robley, Watts's booker and JYD's partner for the tag team titles. Inside the office, Watts and Robley were having problems that would lead to Robley's departure. For one, Watts believed Robley had a substance-abuse issue. Another, perhaps in business terms even bigger, problem was what one might call a booker's ego. Generally speaking, active wrestlers made for lousy bookers, because they tended to put the shine on themselves, often at the expense of the territory they worked for and the talent they were supposed to be pushing. Watts said he felt like Robley wanted everything to revolve around Robley. He was, after all, involved in the

Junkyard Dog's feud with the Freebirds, both at the Superdome show and in the arenas.

In some ways Robley's turn on the Junkyard Dog was atypical of the soon-to-be-pattern. For one thing, it didn't lead to a big Superdome show. It was more of a last hurrah for a worker with great talent who was near the end of his career. JYD had, in fact, already moved on to new partners. On November 27, 1980, at the 'Dome, JYD teamed with the retiring Watts to beat Ladd and "Bad" Leroy Brown. Then, on April, 18, 1981, he teamed up with Murdoch to enter a tag team tournament for the vacant titles. The show drew 22,000 fans, almost as much as the Freebird feud. The main draw was the first-time team of Mid South's two biggest babyfaces, which was pushed as a great step forward in race relations, the Civil Rights Act of the wrestling world.

The pairing may have solved all the problems of race, but it didn't net JYD and Murdoch, or "Captain Redneck," the titles. They did beat the Freebirds, who were flown in from Atlanta for the big show, and Ladd and Brown; however, they lost in the finals to the masked duo of the Grappler and the Super Destroyer. Before the next Superdome Spectacular, JYD and Murdoch would capture the titles. To show how far Robley had fallen, he teamed with Cocoa Samoa and lost to the Freebirds in the first round. He would soon claim that JYD had turned his back on him and make a final heel turn. The blow-off came quickly. Robley didn't rate much of a feud. Perhaps, in reality, it was Watts who had turned his back on Robley.

When the next 'Dome show came, in July, it was indeed a revenge match for JYD against an ex-friend. This time it was Paul Orndorff. Initially, it wasn't even JYD that Orndorff turned heel on. However, the formula was in place. The turn came right in line with the big show. The ex-friend claimed to be overlooked, said he was tired of being mis-treated, and desired a title shot. In the beginning, through interference and cheating, the new heel would have some measure of success. In the end, however, revenge would belong to JYD.

Orndorff had started wrestling in 1977, the same year as JYD. The two had similar backgrounds. Like JYD, Orndorff had a good career in college football at a small school, and was unsuccessful in the pro ranks. In Orndorff's case, he played running back for the University of Tampa, scoring 21 touchdowns and netting more than 2,000 all-purpose yards. He was drafted by the New Orleans Saints, but he didn't make the team. He did play a season with the Jacksonville Sharks of the World Football League, but by the next year he had left football behind for wrestling. Orndorff was a childhood friend of Mike Graham, son of Watts's mentor, the legendary Florida promoter Eddie Graham, so he had an open path into wrestling. He trained with Hiro Matsuda and former NWA champ Jack Brisco and achieved quick success, headlining almost immediately in Memphis against Jerry Lawler.

Tri-State started using Orndorff in 1978, and he did well in his initial run. He won the North American title that year, beating Ladd for the belt both times. However, his reigns were short, more to establish him as a champion than to be the defending champ. He quickly lost the title back to Ladd on each occasion.

Orndorff frequently main evented for Tri-State and Mid South. On the August 2, 1980, card he wrestled fifth from the top, beating Ken Mantell. On the next 'Dome show, the November card in which Watts teamed with JYD to beat Ladd and Brown, Orndorff's lights out match — or a match that was billed as unsanctioned by the promotion and therefore had no rules — with Ladd was the main event.

In the summer of 1981, the Grappler held the North American title; Orndorff was one of his top challengers, and was closing in. He had a scheduled title shot in Shreveport on the television show, but "overslept," and missed the match. In his place, Jake Roberts stepped up and took the title. When Orndorff showed up, he expressed his frustration at being upstaged and losing his shot at the title. That angle led to a more aggressive Orndorff, who first roughed up his overmatched

JYD versus Orndorff.

opponents, then turned on his friends. He turned on Roberts and challenged him to a title match. A short time later, JYD tried to reason with Orndorff. For his trouble, he was attacked, as well. Both grudges led to the Superdome.

On July 4, 1981, 18,000 fans paid to see Orndorff battle not once, but twice against his former friends. It wasn't at all uncommon for a headliner to wrestle twice on a big show, in Mid South or anywhere else, especially if he had more than one feud or title on the line. For instance, JYD often wrestled in a tag team title match in addition to wrestling to settle a main-event feud. He would do so on this card, as well, teaming with Murdoch to defend the tag team belts against the Wild Samoans, who were managed by Ladd. Orndorff also had two big matches on that 4th of July. Independent of his babyface image, he had a title shot against Roberts and a main event against JYD. The grudge match against JYD was also billed as a lights out match, and because lights out matches were unsanctioned, titles were not on the line. That meant something big on this occasion.

In the title match, Orndorff defeated Roberts for the North American title. When the Junkyard Dog beat Orndorff in the main event, he didn't win the belt. He did become the top contender, however, scoring a pinfall win over the new champ. It was a nice, logical piece of booking that ensured the summer would be filled up with JYD chasing the gold. He wouldn't win it right away. Orndorff managed to elude him, even though he never defeated him cleanly. For JYD, who Watts had booked to be a star without the big belt, the chase for the title had begun in earnest. It would continue for the greater part of a year. When the time came to move the title from Orndorff, the win went to Ted DiBiase at New Orleans' Municipal Auditorium in November.

Orndorff stayed in Mid South for a few more months, and eventually returned to the babyface side. The angle neatly paralleled his heel turn. He had a title shot scheduled against DiBiase, but had "car trouble." Former Olympic Greco-Roman wrestler Bob Roop took the match and beat the champ. Later, when Orndorff made it to the television studio, Roop gloated that he was the one who had sabotaged Orndorff's car. Orndorff turned on Roop, to the cheers of the fans, though he didn't regain the strap.

Behind the scenes, Watts had tired of Orndorff, and had labeled him a malcontent who was always unhappy about his position on the card, his angle, or, most importantly, his paychecks. Watts claimed that he even switched to paying his talent after, rather than prior to, the taping of the television interviews because Orndorff's displeasure affected his promos. Finally, Orndorff's displeasure spilled over and he left for good. He became a headliner for the Georgia territory for a year, then, in 1983, he became one of the many wrestlers who simply disappeared for a time, only to turn up in the WWF just as it began its national expansion. He headlined the first WWF WrestleMania in 1985, then set a North American attendance record in 1986 for a match in Toronto against Hulk Hogan.

Back in Mid South, JYD continued to chase gold until 1982. He defeated Roop on June 21, 1982, at the Dog's Yard in New Orleans. It was the culmination of a long program. The problem with such a chase angle is that crowds tend to shrink after the payoff. While some fluctuations were expected, even encouraged within well-run territories, no one wanted business to cool down. Watts and Ladd knew they needed a hot angle to keep ticket sales flowing, and were searching for a big heel to be groomed for the next run at JYD. However, they had fed all of their standard heels to JYD in his buildup, so they were coming up empty. Further, because they booked JYD in short, decisive matches in which he squashed heels in less than two minutes, they had a hard time using a regular for the spot. So, they began a national search and solicited opinions from their friends.

Ladd mentioned the problem to DiBiase, and asked him to keep his eyes open. DiBiase was a second-generation wrestler, the son of female wrestler Helen Hild and stepson of "Iron" Mike DiBiase. He had become a solid, respected worker, and, with his recent North American title reign, he had climbed into one of the top spots as a babyface in Mid South, which was realistically as far as he could go under JYD.

He had also become a national attraction, doing a stint in New York for the WWF and growing into a headliner in St. Louis. Because of his national exposure, Ladd thought he might have some insight into a hot new bad-guy attraction for Mid South. Shortly thereafter, DiBiase came up with a wrestler.

As DiBiase wrote in *The Million Dollar Man*, "One night in Shreveport, I went to visit Ernie at his hotel room at the Sheraton. We chit-chatted and then I told him I had found the perfect heel. His eyes lit up and he wanted to know the name of the wrestler. In an excited manner, I said, 'Ernie, you are looking at him!' Ernie smiled and his eyes got as big as pumpkins. He started shaking his fingers at me and said, 'Why didn't I think of that? That's it!'"

Turning DiBiase made a lot of sense. Everyone knew he'd gone as far as he could as a face in Mid South. To the fans, DiBiase was one of JYD's sidekicks, and that would never change. The promotion knew it would likely have to send him to another territory once he outgrew the second-fiddle act. Instead, they could make him into a headliner, equal to his footing outside of Mid South. The realism behind the angle meant the interviews would practically write themselves. DiBiase, who was growing disenchanted with being seen as number two to JYD, had to do something to get the success he felt he deserved. As a fierce competitor, he couldn't let himself be stifled, even by friendship.

Outside the ring, DiBiase and JYD really were great friends, another fact most everyone seemed to know. They were neighbors in Baton Rouge, frequent travelling companions, and, to the extent JYD trained, workout partners. When DiBiase got married on New Year's Eve, 1981, JYD was his best man. When DiBiase turned, it meant unbelievable heat. He hadn't just gone to the dark side for money and titles. He had betrayed his best friend.

Shortly before the big angle, DiBiase "injured" his hand. To keep wrestling with the injury, he took to wearing a wrap to keep the hand protected. DiBiase's black glove would become one of the most infamous, and successful, gimmicks in wrestling over the next four years. But the glove would come later; at first, it was basic protective tape, but the effect would be the same.

On June 23, 1982, just two days after JYD won the title, DiBiase went on television and challenged his friend to a match. He explained that he had been the champion a mere three months earlier, and had been chasing Roop ever since he lost the title. Because he was the previous champion, he felt he deserved to be the top contender. It wouldn't be fair, he felt, for him to be denied a title shot simply because both men were fan favorites, or even because of their friendship. Although the promotion might have balked at such a match, JYD agreed. He explained that he thought DiBiase deserved the match, and, as the new champion, he wanted to defend against the best competitors. The match would happen that very day, right there in Shreveport, and would be shown on television.

The bout began, as wrestling cliché demands, with the two babyfaces shaking hands. From there, it followed the familiar form of the heel turn. The two men locked up twice, and each time JYD overpowered DiBiase, pushing him back into the ropes. DiBiase's frustration grew. Next, each man used a surprise roll-up to get a simple one-count. Back to standing, the two men circled warily, adjusting to the fact that a good friend was now the opponent. Next, they traded an inconclusive series of scientific moves, with neither of them gaining an advantage. At the end of the series, JYD gave DiBiase a snapmare and went to hit him with a fist drop. Normally, that would have been JYD's typical sequence of events. This time he stopped himself, not wanting to hit his friend with a clenched fist. A moment later, however, DiBiase backed JYD into the ropes, and, breaking the rules for the first time, did indeed hit him with a fist. JYD didn't sell the punch, and instead decked DiBiase with a return volley. Next, the two men traded two-counts, JYD after hitting a Russian leg sweep and DiBiase after a big powerslam. Although JYD kicked out, DiBiase pressed his advantage and put on a submission move, the spinning toe hold made famous by his trainers, the Funk Brothers. JYD kicked out of the move, and DiBiase went flying over the top rope. Normally, this would be grounds for disqualification in Mid South, but the referee ruled that JYD had not intended for DiBiase to go over the rope. Outside the ring, JYD and the referee helped DiBiase get to his feet. JYD rolled his friend back into the ring, but he and the referee were both slow to return. During the delay, DiBiase pulled a foreign object from his trunks, loaded it into his hand protection and knocked JYD out cold with one punch. A three-count later, DiBiase had regained the title. JYD's reign had only been a matter of days; it was a very stunning, but sly segue from a climactic title chase into a new, heated feud.

The Superdome Spectacular took place two weeks later, and drew 22,800 fans, second only to the match with Hayes back in 1980. JYD, trying to gain revenge on DiBiase, was added to the card late, which drew a huge walk-up crowd. The promotion didn't want to end the feud too early, so the match went on third to last, and ended in a double disqualification. To send the fans home happy, in the main event JYD and Mr. Olympia successfully defended their tag team titles against the Super Destroyer and Big John Studd, who were the Georgia tag team champs at the time, and were regularly seen on the WTBS Superstation cable show. The feud with DiBiase would continue throughout the territory for the rest of the summer.

In the fall, a new twist for Mid South gave JYD versus DiBiase another six months of juice. DiBiase had started a stable of heel wrestlers called the Rat Pack, and as their leader had dubbed himself the Big Cheese. Among the wrestlers was "Hacksaw" Jim Duggan and "Maniac" Matt Borne. Borne and DiBiase challenged JYD and Olympia for the tag team belts. The feud became as heated as the Dog-DiBiase singles matches. The heels challenged the champs to a title shot that coincided with the county fair in Shreveport. There were major stipulations: not only would the titles be on the line, but the man who was pinned would have to leave town for 90 days.

Loser-leaves-town matches were popular blowoff stipulations for ending feuds. They were often used when one wrestler was actually leaving a territory, or had given his notice, and was staying behind simply to put over the other wrestlers for the sake of the business. In Florida, Dusty Rhodes had come up with a new way of booking the match. Since fans had grown to expect the babyface to win such climactic events, Rhodes booked himself to lose such a match — albeit against massive interference. The heels ganged up on him, and the promotion was billed as being against him because it was unable or unwilling to take a stand against the illegal act. So, Rhodes booked himself as a masked avenger, the Midnight Rider. The heels cried foul, but the Midnight Rider rode into town and gained revenge. He even won the NWA World Title, but had to give it back because of an obscure rule that a masked man would have to unmask if he won the championship. This twist on the loser-leaves-town match was popular in Florida, at least until Rhodes ran it into the ground by using it too often. Watts, looking for a way to keep his top feud going, decided to give it a try, too.

As the tag team match started, fans had every reason to expect success. Not only were JYD and Olympia having a great reign — six months and counting since they had defeated the Samoans — but DiBiase's henchman, Duggan, had been barred from ringside. If anyone suspected a title change, they still probably figured that it would be the masked Mr. Olympia who would suffer the loss and have to leave town. After all, it seemed like JYD's various partners were always the ones who did the losing on the rare occasions the good guys lost. Still, few suspected a loss for the champs.

Spirits were high for the fair. Even a costumed gorilla from the fairgrounds took in the matches. The gorilla turned out to be Duggan in disguise. He gave JYD his trademark finishing maneuver, the spear, and his mask came off, revealing the trick. JYD suffered the pinfall, the Rat Pack won the titles, and Mid South lost its hero for 90 days.

Of course, JYD didn't actually leave. Instead, Watts created an alter ego, the masked Stagger Lee. Casual fans, even traditional wrestling fans from around the country, may have missed the symbolism, but JYD's fans in the black community got the meaning loud and clear. The story of Stagger Lee was popular, made legendary in dozens of songs by some of the biggest musicians over the course of a century. In 1895, "Stagger" Lee Shelton, a carriage driver and alleged pimp, stabbed his friend Billy Lyons to death on a St. Louis street. Shelton was black, and Lyons was white. The incident was a sensation in the newspaper tabloids. A couple of decades later, "Mississippi" John Hurt recorded a ballad about the killing. The song became a type of anthem, especially in the black community. Over the years, the song was re-recorded by many popular acts, including Fats Domino; the Isley Brothers; Ma Rainey; Pat Boone; Neil Diamond; Bill Haley and the Comets; Southside Johnny and the Asbury Jukes; the Grateful Dead; and Huey Lewis and the News. More recently, Beck did a version of the song. According to his Wikipedia entry, Stagger Lee became a symbol, "an archetype, the embodiment of a tough black man, one who is sly, streetwise, cool, lawless, amoral, potentially violent and who defies white authority." For a black babyface who had been wronged by his friend and banned by his promotion, it was the perfect gimmick.

Stagger Lee showed up in Mid South the week after the tag team match. His outfit looked almost identical to JYD's, although he wore a full bodysuit. His mask couldn't quite hide his features. Of course, the Rat Pack protested. Watts and the announcers sold the injustice of JYD's loss instead, and winked at the possibility of him flouting the rules. If the Rat Pack could prove it was JYD, the story line went, then

JYD would be suspended for life. However, the one time they finally got the drop on the mystery man and unmasked him, he turned out to be good old Ray Candy.

The 'Dome show was on November 25, 1982, one month after the tag team match. More than 15,000 fans saw JYD, that is, Stagger Lee, gain revenge on DiBiase and capture the North American title. Soon, DiBiase dropped a loser-leaves-town match, because he was heading for a stint closer to home, in Georgia. After a big year, the feud was temporarily over, and all was well in Mid South, for a moment, anyway.

When DiBiase returned, he had an even bigger feud, this time with his former partner, Duggan. He continued to wrestle for Watts for several more years, eventually working the territory while also becoming a headliner on Japanese tours. In 1986, while he was still a heel, DiBiase was set for an NWA World Title shot against Ric Flair. While he was on his way to the ring, he was attacked by a jealous Dick Murdoch and almost missed the match. By the time he wrestled, bandaged up and bleeding a river, he would be Mid South's biggest babyface once more. He lost because of Murdoch's attack, but he won his people back, four years after he had become the territory's most reviled villain. He stayed with Watts for another year, through the name change to the Universal Wrestling Federation (UWF) and the attempt to go national. He feuded with the Freebirds and engaged in a bloody series with Michael Hayes. When Watts sold out to Crockett, DiBiase jumped to the WWF. He may have arrived late, but he made up for lost time. As the Million Dollar Man, he became a national headliner, and for a time he was once again the hottest heel in the country.

Stagger Lee mysteriously left Mid South just as the Junkyard Dog's suspension ended. With the North American title vacant, JYD returned and the promotion pushed him as the obvious favorite to win the tournament to crown a new champ. It was held in his backyard, the Downtown Municipal Auditorium in New Orleans. It looked like JYD would finally get his title reign, but things weren't so simple, and there was another Superdome show coming up. This time, Mr. Olympia got the honors.

Jerry Stubbs had been a headliner in Southern promotions for several years, especially in his home state of Alabama. He had above-average skills as a talker and very good skills as a worker. What he didn't have was a great look. He did have a nice, perhaps chemically enhanced, physique. However, he was an average-looking, balding, average-sized guy, the kind of guy you might see yelling "Roll Tide!" at a University of Alabama football game, not the kind of guy who would make you turn your head at the airport and say "Wow, he must be a wrestler." Perhaps for that reason he never went much further than the Deep South, and never had a national run. However, in his home state, or under the mask as Mr. Olympia, he was solid, especially when he was carrying the action for or against the Junkyard Dog.

Like JYD in 1982, Olympia had lost a loser-leaves-town match. At the time, he was teamed with Lee against the Rat Pack. When he returned, he expressed dismay over being displaced, only not directly at JYD. Much as Orndorff started his turn with someone other than JYD, Olympia's initial turn came at the expense of another wrestler, in this case Johnny Walker, a.k.a. Mr. Wrestling II. Walker had been a huge babyface for nearly a decade, and had only recently made his return from Georgia. As the story line went, Mr. Wrestling II noticed that his pure white masks were being defaced. He caught Olympia with a suitcase full of stolen masks; Olympia said he had done it because he wanted to be the top masked man in the territory. The Olympia turn collided with JYD's title chase and the tournament in New Orleans. Using interference, Olympia had JYD down on his stomach, but the referee, who was groggy after being struck accidentally, counted the pinfall that wasn't, and mistakenly awarded the title to Olympia.

At the next television taping, Watts appeared with the title belt and gave one of his world-according-to-Bill-Watts speeches to explain that Mid South was investigating the referee's decision. While the belt shouldn't go to a man who didn't really win the title, it also couldn't go to the man the official declared the loser. Olympia had taken on the hated "Arab" Skandar Akbar as his manager, and therefore had access to a host of lawyers that worked for Akbar. Watts seemed to fear or dislike lawyers so much himself that he always projected it onto his audience; every bad guy seemed to have better counsel and more lawyers than the babyfaces could possibly afford. Since Akbar was an "oil barron" he had the best lawyers. As Watts prefaced each situation, he would say to the announcer, Boyd Pierce, "Boyd, you know how lawyers are." To resolve the situation and avoid litigation, Mid South decided to hold the title up until JYD and Olympia could settle things in the ring at the Superdome. On April 16, 1983, they did just that, and JYD beat Olympia in a steel cage to win the North American title back. The official attendance was 21,400, better than the November show with Stagger Lee, and the best attendance in what turned out to be a down year for the promotion.

On the undercard, Butch Reed, who was billed as a young, up-and-coming star, defeated the Black Ninja, a Japanese wrestler known in other places as Kendo Nagasaki. A former NFL running back, Bruce Reed had come up in Missouri and been a breakout star in Florida and Georgia before catching on in Mid South. He would be pushed as a black protégé for the Junkyard Dog. When he turned on JYD that summer, he therefore became one of his most hated rivals. Although both would have other programs over the next year, JYD and Reed kept coming back to fight each other, much as JYD and DiBiase had the previous year. In the end, although Reed won very few of their matches, Watts would try to sell to his crowds that it was the "pressure put on him by Butch Reed" that finally made JYD crack and leave for less stressful competition.

Originally, Reed looked to be the one who had cracked. He had been a solid mid-card babyface for his first months in the territory, pushing toward the top, or at least the spot behind JYD. He had even won a "battle of the Hacksaws" against Jim Duggan. However, when Duggan made a face turn on his Rat Pack partner DiBiase, Reed found himself pushed down a rung. The breaking point came when the fans picked Duggan, and not Reed, to be JYD's partner to challenge DiBiase and Olympia for the tag team titles. Reed gave an interview that sounded a lot like the interviews given by Orndorff, DiBiase, and Olympia. He said he was tired of being passed over, and needed to start looking out for himself. JYD came to confront him, and the two men were soon in battle.

In a twist, Reed challenged JYD at the Superdome Spectacular on July 16, 1983. While the attendance figures have been lost over time, it was not the best 'Dome draw, perhaps because the match, strictly speaking, wasn't about JYD's revenge. The bout itself went old school, in that it was scheduled for two out of three falls. Reed made this demand because he claimed that JYD wasn't the same caliber of athlete, and couldn't hang with him in an extended contest. Of course, as the match went on, it was Reed who looked to be out of his league The first two falls were inconclusive, with each man winning one by disqualification. Reed won his when JYD's anger got the better of him, and he uncharacteristically broke the rules. JYD won his when the first flurry of outside interference began. First, "Maddog" Buzz Sawyer interfered. As JYD ran Sawyer off, the referee got in the way and was knocked out. King Kong Bundy appeared fresh from defeating Dusty Rhodes in a taped-fist match. With Reed also out cold from the second fall, Bundy used his taped fists to knock out JYD. Bundy then dragged Reed onto JYD, revived the ref, and the title changed hands. For JYD's fans, it was the only conceivable way he could lose. In interviews, Reed sold it as if he had proven himself as the Olympic wrestling champion. Of course, this only angered JYD and his fans even more.

The Junkyard Dog's revenge came in stages. On one hand, he dominated Reed every time they crossed paths. On the other hand, he wouldn't win the title back for months. The promotion even did an angle toward the end of the initial run in which Reed refused to put the title on the line against JYD, claiming that he had already given him all the chances he deserved. Reed then picked Terry Allen, a.k.a. Magnum T.A., to get the title shot, instead. Allen was Dusty Rhodes's real-life protégé, an up-and-coming heartthrob and a former tag team champ with Duggan.

With an assist from JYD, T.A. stunned the Shreveport audience by defeating Reed and taking the gold. Twelve days later, in New Orleans, T.A. took an unsanctioned challenge from the Russian strongman Nikolai Volkoff and lost the belt. Mid South intervened and stripped Volkoff of the title. Watts gave an interview in which he explained that Volkoff couldn't be the champ because the match was unsanctioned, and T.A. had violated the rules by granting it and therefore was stripped of the title. As the last two legally sanctioned champs, Reed and the Junkyard Dog would vie for the held-up title. They brought in Rhodes as the guest referee, and JYD regained the belt in October.

Perhaps it was the odd booking, perhaps it was a stale group of headliners, or perhaps it was just the normal ups and downs of a territory, but business was on its ass at this point. The November 'Dome show, booked as a five-match card with JYD beating Reed on top to settle the feud, drew just 8,000 fans. The undercards had star power, including Dusty Rhodes, the Von Erichs, and the hot new tag team from the Georgia territory, the Road Warriors, but there were no local angles besides the main event. At the same time, the Junkyard Dog and Reed seemed like a settled feud; the JYD already had his revenge. In the last years of the federation, especially the days after it became the UWF, 8,000 fans was about the norm. In November 1983, it was unimaginable.

Ultimately, it wasn't the Junkyard Dog and Reed who bore the brunt of the blame for the poor show or the smaller crowds. In the spring of 1984, Reed and JYD had another run. This time, Reed had help from a sidekick/lackey, "Nature Boy" Buddy Landel. Landel had been an opening-match good guy in 1982, when he was JYD's neighbor and driving partner. Now, he returned with a small push as Reed's sneaky, cowardly best friend. He drew great heat with his act; he was always quick to kick an opponent that Reed had taken care of, and even quicker to run and hide behind Reed when that opponent made a comeback. Together, Reed and Landel put some fire back into the feud and it had another good run. They added more of a personal twist to the feud, too, as Sonny King, JYD's trainer, came into the federation and took all sorts of abuse from Reed and Landel to heat up the issue.

It was this run that JYD walked out on to go to the WWF. Although he had won most of the matches, especially the specialty matches designed as blowoffs, after the fact Watts sold it to his audience as if Reed had been the true winner. Since JYD broke traditional wrestling protocol and disappeared without giving notice, or without staying behind and "doing business," or losing to the wrestlers who were staying, for four to six weeks it did look as if he had run away from the grudge matches. Reed and JYD did have one final Superdome match, on June 16, 1984, drawing 21,700 fans and a gate of $166,000. True to form, JYD beat Reed again, this time in Reed's specialty match, the Ghetto Street Fight.

Over the years, Ritter's feuds and angles had not been free of racial overtones. His initial push was as a black superhero, some of his mannerisms could be called stereotypical, and his tag team with Murdoch was pushed as a step forward in race relations. When white partners turned on him, whether it was Robley, Orndorff, DiBiase, or Olympia, there's no doubt the feuds carried, subconsciously if not always overtly, racial implications. At the same time, JYD had feuds with several black wrestlers in which race could be an issue. Ladd could make an interview a pointed dissertation on race, or anything else for that matter. JYD also had a feud with a Mississippi native named James Harris who found a career by playing an African savage, Kamala the Ugandan Giant. However, the feud with Reed touched on race and racial issues more directly than any other time in JYD's Mid South run.

From the beginning, Reed portrayed the Junkyard Dog as a sellout, touching on images of JYD as the house slave, the minstrel show act, and the dregs of society. During the later run, Reed and Landel attempted to tar and feather JYD with molasses. The climactic matches were the Ghetto Street Fights, a variation of the Texas Death Match. "Butch Reed, we've fought in every room in the house," JYD would say, "now it's time to take it out to the street." It's hard to say what nerve this touched in the fans. A white partner turning on JYD stoked one form of anger. A black protégé turning heel in the worst possible manner stoked an even deeper rage. A parallel exists in the real world. Harassment and mistreatment from the white community is cause for outrage, but historically, it has been expected. Black-on-black crime, however, is viewed with horror and sorrow.

It is also worth noting, again, the explanation of stereotypes in wrestling, how they were designed to play out in booking, and how they actually did play out in Mid South. As Terry Funk once said, of course the bad guy is a German, or Japanese, or an Arab, a racist, a womanizer, or just your garden-variety cheater. In the end, the bad guy gets his. Reed turned on JYD and called him every name in the book (short of the N-word, anyway). At the end of almost every match, 99 times out of 100, JYD beat the tar out of Reed. The next week, Reed came back running his mouth again, and the result was the same. Speaking of tar, even if the angle made people uncomfortable, the payoff of that angle was that cowardly Buddy Landel looked hysterical covered in molasses and feathers. Ultimately, it was up to the viewer, and is now up to the reader, to decide what to think. It would be wrong, however, to ignore this part of the history of the Junkyard Dog.

Between Reed's two feuds with JYD came two other big angles for Mid South. JYD was a major player in both, although neither featured him in the lead role. One involved another famous turn, although it would be the least successful of the bunch. The other involved a cowardly sneak even more effective than Landel, plus the return of the Cowboy. One ended up being the most successful angle in Mid South history. The other killed New Orleans as a top wrestling market. They called the big angle the Last Stampede. The name alluded to the return of Bill Watts to the squared circle, but it also marked the end of the era of the Junkyard Dog.

CHAPTER SEVEN

THE LAST STAMPEDE

"Rubber Man" Johnny Walker had never been a main-event star. Despite his many years in wrestling, his ability on the mic, his fire, and his skill in the ring, his gimmick never caught on. One of the great things about the old territory system, however, is that a wrestler could move on and find another gimmick. In fact, he could go from the opening match or mid-card to the top of the bill with the right change in look, name, or idea, or with a little bit of seasoning and the right mix of opponents, fans, and bookings. That's what happened in the early

'70s, when Walker put on simple white trunks and a white mask and became Mr. Wrestling II.

The original Mr. Wrestling, Tim Woods, had been a Georgia favorite. The idea was for Mr. Wrestling II to feud with the original. The gimmick worked so well that soon the masked men were both favorites and an occasional tag team. On his own, Mr. Wrestling II caught fire, and for the next decade he was a masked headliner. While he enjoyed fame in the ring, his biggest national attention came when Georgian Jimmy Carter ran for president. Carter's mom was a huge wrestling fan, and Mr. Wrestling II was her favorite. Carter had a folksy, homespun appeal, and the tie to wrestling helped. In one of the most famous pictures in professional wrestling history, Carter put a headlock on Mr. Wrestling II. When Carter was elected, he invited Mr. Wrestling II to the inauguration. The wrestler planned to attend. However, when he learned that he would have to go without his mask, he politely declined.

A little less than a decade later, in 1983, Johnny Walker's career was winding down. Because of his mask, few fans could guess his age, but he was in his fifties. He had already been in wrestling for twenty years before he donned the hood for another decade. His return to Mid South featured several tag team title reigns, as well as big feuds with Mr. Olympia and Kamala. Crowds loved him, chanting, "II, II, II," whenever he was down, and even more when he began gaining momentum to set up his finisher, "the million dollar kneelift." He even got a title shot against American Wrestling Association World Champion Nick Bockwinkle in Houston for promoter Paul Boesch.

As with any babyface in Mid South not named Junkyard Dog, Mr. Wrestling II could only climb so high. He could win tag team titles, have hot feuds, and be a solid number two — pun intended — but he couldn't be the top guy. Because of his age, it probably wouldn't have been a good idea, anyway. Of course, being a solid number two had its drawbacks, as well. If the top guys never changed, things would get

*The legendary match with Mr. Wrestling that marked
the end of New Orleans as a hotbed of wrestling.*

stale. Since JYD wasn't going anywhere — at least in Watts's mind —
other guys had to come and go, rise and fall. When business fell off in
late 1983, a shake-up was desperately needed.

Late in the year, Watts invited Memphis promoter Jerry Jarrett and his partner and main-event star Jerry Lawler to visit the territory to help him solve the problem. Memphis had been a successful promotion over the years due to its frugal approach and the fact that its lead star was a co-owner. It was also on the cutting edge in its use of music videos to make new stars. Jarrett and Lawler attended a television taping and a couple of shows, and had a surprising response to Watts's problems. They asked him: "Where are all the blow jobs?"

Although he would flirt with, and eventually develop, a relationship with Christianity, back in the day Watts was no angel. Still, he reacted to Jarrett and Lawler with anger. He wasn't a pimp. If they wanted blow jobs, they could get them themselves. Hilarity ensued. Jarrett and Lawler explained to Watts that they meant young, female fans. Watts, having promoted a territory of big, tough guys wrestling in "real," athletic contests — that is, like McGuirk before him and many other promoters, having promoted a version of his own wrestling career — hadn't considered attracting a different fan base with a different style of wrestler. His fans were older, blue-collar men and women, and with JYD's success, he also had legions of black fans. Meanwhile, with the Von Erichs in Dallas, Tommy Rich in Georgia, Ricky Steamboat in the Mid Atlantic, and the Fabulous Ones in Memphis, promotions were luring in teenage girls to see the hot, young male stars with sleek, cut (and steroid-enhanced) bodies. With the young girls came the young guys. If you added that formula to Watts's crowds, as Memphis had already done, you turned a half-filled arena into a sellout.

Watts traded some heels he had run out of ideas for, King Kong Bundy chief among them, for a group of younger, good-looking baby-faces named Terry Taylor, Ricky Morton, and Robert Gibson. Morton and Gibson had formed a tag team called the Rock 'n' Roll Express, which had always been stuck behind the Fabulous Ones in Memphis. Watts also got two mid-card wrestlers, Bobby Eaton and Dennis

Condrey, to put together as a heel tag team, that would be known as the Midnight Express. All these acquisitions turned out to be successful. However, the biggest piece of the puzzle may have been Jim Cornette, the outspoken 21-year-old photographer turned manager. As with Morton and Gibson, despite his obvious talent, Cornette was stuck behind Memphis mainstay Jimmy Hart. Together with new booker Bill Dundee, a Memphis headliner who had grown stale in his home territory, the new additions began to pop the territory as 1984 began.

Terry Allen fit the new philosophy perfectly, too. Dusty Rhodes had been grooming him for several years to be the next big babyface in wrestling. In the ring, Allen resembled Tom Selleck's character in *Magnum P.I.*, due to his mustache and biker-boy good looks, so Rhodes nicknamed him Magnum T.A. Rhodes gave T.A. a big push in Florida, then sent him to Watts for some out-of-territory seasoning. Later, when Rhodes jumped from Florida to the old Mid Atlantic territory and promoter Jim Crockett took control of the NWA banner and expanded to it into a national company, Rhodes intended to push T.A. all the way to the world title. In 1983, Watts simply wanted to help Rhodes turn T.A. into a main eventer. He started by first making him tag team champ with Duggan, and again with Mr. Wrestling II. Then he booked the aborted title switch with Reed. The reality was that Watts didn't want T.A. to hold the title; he just wanted to establish him as viable in the fans' eyes. Allen defeated Reed with help from the Junkyard Dog, who served as a biased special referee. Soon after, Allen lost the title in an unsanctioned defense against Nikolai Volkoff. The plan was to make a big program out of T.A. chasing the championship, hoping to avenge his earlier mistake, which Watts chalked up to youthful hotheadedness. Therefore, the chase for the North American belt would symbolically be about Magnum T.A. gaining maturity.

With the story line in place, it made perfect sense to involve the legendary veteran, Mr. Wrestling II. On Christmas night at the Dog's Yard in New Orleans, T.A. and Mr. Wrestling II won the tag team titles from Butch Reed and Jim Neidhart. Watts and his announcers sold the pairing as teacher and student, but it would be an uncomfortable relationship. Slowly, subtly, Mr. Wrestling II turned into the jealous mentor, upset that his young pupil was outshining him. At first, it was just the inflection in his voice. Then it was his body language. Finally, they began showing training sessions in which Mr. Wrestling II would berate T.A. for seemingly minor, or even invisible, mistakes. In one training session, he went so far as to slap T.A. because he lacked focus. By March, the relationship had completely broken down.

At the same time, Mr. Wrestling II started issuing challenges to the Junkyard Dog for the North American title. The interviews followed the familiar pattern. Mr. Wresting II felt overlooked. As a legend in the territory, he felt that he deserved a title shot, no matter who held the title. If he had to wrestle a fellow fan favorite, like JYD, he didn't mind. He claimed to be insulted that JYD and Mid South never offered him the opportunity. JYD insisted that Mid South set the matches, and he had no problem wrestling his friend. He agreed that Mr. Wrestling II deserved a shot, but stated that he knew he could defeat the masked man. If he didn't, JYD added, he would leave Mid South for 90 days.

Mr. Wrestling II was loved, but very few people thought he would defeat JYD. Certainly, he would never do so at the Dog's Yard in New Orleans. Watts and Dundee must have figured that such a loss would draw massive heat. In a way, they were right. On March 12, 1984, at the Municipal Auditorium, Mr. Wrestling II loaded his kneepad with a foreign object and knocked JYD out to win the title. In the mold of DiBiase's turn, the match was designed to be a classic that would end with a similar, controversial finish. At the very least, it did end in controversy. After a slow, plodding affair, Mr. Wrestling II loaded his knee. Normally, his opponents leaned into the move, making it look like they had taken one right in the kisser. This time, JYD was out of position, and Mr. Wrestling II grazed him in the chest. It looked awful.

When JYD sold it as if he had been coldcocked and got pinned, the boos rained down. For an audience that had been trained to suspend its disbelief, the finish was a slap in the face. Their hero, the man who was unbeatable in that arena, had just gone down to a missed move. To them, either JYD threw the match or wrestling really was fake. The heat was incredible — in the wrong way. Many of the fans left the arena that night and never returned. The next week, attendance dropped by half. By the summer, Mid South had switched to a different venue in New Orleans, the Lakefront Arena at the University of New Orleans in suburban Lakeview. Just before the move, the promotion stopped running weekly shows in the city. Just like that, New Orleans was ruined as a wrestling town.

Mr. Wrestling II's heel turn bombed. The next day in Lafayette, Louisiana, he walked out on T.A. in a tag team defense against the Midnight Express. Despite his valiant efforts, T.A. couldn't fight off the Express by himself; he got pinned and lost the titles. He then started his quest for the singles title against his ex-mentor.

While T.A. was a big hit with the new crowd of young girls, he did not get similar adoration from the old-school fans. In many places, Mr. Wrestling II was cheered and T.A. was booed. The promotion tried its hardest, even pushing a name change, with Mr. Wrestling II claiming he was now the original Mr. Wrestling. He even brought out a new protégé, Ray Fernandez, a steroided-up muscle man who wore the traditional white trunks and mask, and renamed him Mr. Wrestling II. The pro wrestling magazines had a field day with the name switch, and defended the honor of the Mr. Wrestling name for Tim Woods. But in Mid South, where Tim Woods had never wrestled, there was little heat over it.

T.A. would finally capture the title, but his second reign didn't have the planned pop. He returned to Rhodes before the end of 1984. Over the next two years, he became one of the biggest stars in wrestling for Crockett. He won the United States title, and was being built for a world-title run. He made several big-show returns to Mid South, including several Superdome Spectaculars and matches in Houston, where he challenged for the NWA title. T.A. might have gone on to be a superstar, but his career ended tragically in 1987 when he crashed his Porsche at high speed and suffered career-ending injuries. Mr. Wrestling II's career ended even more quickly. After he dropped the title, the promotion rushed a face turn because of the poor fan reaction. He was damaged goods, however, and he spent his final days in Mid South putting over his new protégé, the new Mr. Wrestling II. Soon enough, the new Mr. Wrestling II was unmasked and revealed to be Hercules Hernandez, who would become Cornette's bodyguard. The original Mr. Wrestling II moved on to Alabama, then jumped to the WWF. His national run was a flop, however, and the WWF only used him as a glorified jobber. He soon retired from wrestling.

By this point, the Junkyard Dog had troubles, too. He was held back by a bad story line in 1983, but outside the ring things had been much worse. Although the twin turns of Olympia and Reed had produced good matches and decent gates at times, much of 1983 had been filled up with battle-of-the-monsters matches with Kamala and the 500-pound Bundy. The formula had always been to put JYD in matches with good workers. Orndorff, DiBiase, Olympia, and Reed could create motion around the slow moving JYD, and were even better at leading him through exciting matches. By contrast, the bouts with Bundy, and especially Kamala, were awful. The longer they went, the worse they got.

Out of the limelight, JYD's partying had become a full-blown cocaine addiction. He stopped training altogether, and his weight ballooned to nearly 350 pounds. He was, quite simply, getting fat. Watts tried to sell it to his audience. "You might have noticed the Junkyard Dog has gained some weight," he said several times on television. "He tells me he had to bulk up to deal with the challenges from super-heavyweights like Kamala and King Kong Bundy." Again, the reality was even worse. Marital problems both led to and fueled the addiction. His wife was eventually committed to a psychiatric institution, and his daughter, La Toya Ritter, moved in with JYD's family. For the most part, she was raised by his grandmother and sister. According to Watts, JYD ended up dating a woman who practiced voodoo. "She would do things that scared him half to death," Watts wrote in his book, "such as burying his clothes in the garden. He was terrified of her — that she had the 'mojo' on him or something. I'm sure the cocaine only aggravated his delusion."

With a month to go before the big spring Superdome show, and with JYD having "left town," a familiar masked man made his return. Stagger Lee's second run would be even more successful than his first, although the gimmick wouldn't be the reason behind the success. Instead, it was the whiny, funny momma's boy, Jim Cornette, and his highlight-machine tag team, the Midnight Express. With the tag team titles wrapped up, and his "birthday" to celebrate, Cornette told the audience in Shreveport and on television that his momma was so happy she sent him a birthday cake, and he was going to have a party. The angle has been done a hundred times now, but when the Rock 'n' Roll Express came out and shoved Cornette's face in the cake, the Mid South audience erupted with laughter. Finally seeing Cornette get what was coming to him was exactly what the crowd wanted. When Mid South went to show it again, however, Cornette threw a temper tantrum. He stormed the announcers and ordered them to stop. Jim Ross told Cornette that the playback came from the truck, where Watts's stepson, Joel, controlled the video.

Cornette started insulting the twenty-something Watts. Then the Cowboy himself, Bill Watts, stepped in. He explained that his stepson was just following his orders, and that he wouldn't put up with anyone speaking ill of him. The elder Watts told Cornette that he would give him a chance to walk away from their argument before it came to blows. Cornette didn't take the advice, and instead tried to put his hands on the Cowboy as he was walking away. Watts turned around and smacked Cornette in the face. Cornette took a huge fall and the crowd went wild for the second time that day.

The next week, the Midnight Express got Cornette's revenge, beating Watts bloody. So began the Last Stampede, billed as Watts's final return to the ring, four years after his retirement. At the April 7, 1984, Superdome Spectacular, Watts and Stagger Lee beat the Midnight Express in a non-title match. Watts blew out his hamstring, but still spent most of the match in the ring so JYD could make the hot tag — once again following the usual formula of avoiding having JYD carry the match himself. Condrey and Eaton were the unsung stars. Every time Watts or JYD touched them, they flew across the ring, carrying the match against two immobile opponents.

The show drew 23,000 fans for Mid South, second only to the JYD-Hayes match in 1980, and a gate of $176,000. However, the Last Stampede did better business overall around the territory. For one thing, Mid South's expansion had added many more markets to the business. When the promotion took over the Tri-State area in 1982, it meant bigger crowds in Oklahoma City and Tulsa, plus all the Arkansas cities. Houston's co-promotion added twice-a-month shows in 1983. Over a two-week period of running the payoff match in every market and getting a sellout or close to a sellout every time, Watts estimated that his business grossed more than a million dollars.

The Junkyard Dog must have earned even more in those weeks than the $12,000 he made back in 1980. Somehow, however, it wasn't enough. His drug problem led to financial problems, as well. The breakup of his marriage pushed him into even more severe drug use. He was one of the best paid wrestlers of the era, and he would continue on that path for the next three years. Still, he wound up broke. When the WWF called and offered him even more money, JYD left Mid South. When the WWF demanded that he leave without giving notice and without "doing business," he simply failed to show up at matches, ruining main events that were scheduled with Reed around the territory. He never talked to Watts or anyone else about his decision. In fact, he didn't see or speak to Watts for nearly a decade afterward.

Initially, Mid South did even better without JYD. In fact, 1984 was the promotion's hottest year, thanks to the packages of Duggan versus DiBiase; the Rock 'n' Roll Express versus the Midnight Express; and handsome wrestlers like Terry Taylor and Magnum T.A. for the girls. In addition, the promotion had a working partnership with the Von Erichs in Dallas. Dundee created one huge angle after another, and almost everything he tried paid off. The newer cities popped big. Duggan versus DiBiase was successful, especially the Tuxedo Death Match angle, which was based on who was the best dressed man in Mid South. In the summer, Watts brought in NWA champ Ric Flair for a series of matches with Kerry Von Erich, based on their quickie title change in April and their rematches from Dallas television. That series did big business, as well. The Midnight Express would eventually move on, but the Rock 'n' Roll Express became huge stars and stayed until the summer of 1985, when they left for Crockett and became huge national stars. All over the territory, things were on fire.

New Orleans was the exception. The March title change marked the end of the sellouts at the Downtown Arena. Within a few weeks, the promotion was filling just a quarter of the seats. In May, it stopped running weekly, and as mentioned, it had moved to the Lakefront Arena by the summer. A hot angle like Duggan-DiBiase might still sell out, as it did on July 27, 1984, but the era of New Orleans being the hottest weekly city for wrestling had ended. The Junkyard Dog and Reed drew the big crowd in June for the Superdome show just before JYD left. In August, Flair and Von Erich drew the last crowd of more than 20,000 wrestling fans at the Superdome. The world title match on August 24, 1984, drew 21,000 and a gate of $165,000. The top Mid South matches were Duggan versus Hernandez and Reed versus T.A. The crowd was noticeably different. JYD's fans were gone, replaced by Von Erich's legion of teenage girls.

Mid South's business slowed in 1985, and the territory suffered a huge blow when the local economy, which was largely based on the oil business, fell off a cliff. Although Mid South had Houston and New Orleans, Oklahoma City and Tulsa, cities that the Central States or Amarillo promotion would have died for, it was suffering in the mid-'80s. Watts always knew that while he had a better territory than some, it wasn't as strong as, say, Vince McMahon's Northeast territory, Crockett's Mid Atlantic, or the Midwest of Verne Gagne's AWA. He had thrived by running better television, giving away more exciting matches, and better story lines that attracted the audience to the arenas to see the resolutions. When the formula worked, it did big business, but when it failed, the business tanked. Worse, again and again McMahon and even Watts's ally, Crockett, picked off his best talent. It wasn't just the Junkyard Dog, it was Duggan, Roberts, Dick Slater, the Rock 'n' Roll Express, Magnum T.A., Kamala, One Man Gang, and anyone else they deemed worth poaching.

Along the way, being known as Mid South hurt Watts badly. When the fledgling sports network ESPN decided to get in on the wrestling boom, it considered Watts, because of his great ratings and slick television. The name scared them off, however, and rather than gamble on a regional thing, they took Verne Gagne's American Wrestling Association (AWA), despite its poor production values and spotty in-ring action. The cable execs didn't understand the difference; they only considered the brand name. Gagne failed miserably in his competition with the WWF, and the AWA eventually stopped promoting. At the end, he had nothing but a television show on ESPN. He ran television programs for a surprisingly long time after he stopped staging house shows, and those old AWA programs air on ESPN Classic to this day.

ESPN also tried wrestling with the remnants of the Dallas and Memphis promotions. Neither of those could match Mid South, either, but at least they got rid of their regional names and became World Class Championship Wrestling and the United States Wrestling Association, respectively.

Of course, ESPN wasn't Watts's first missed opportunity. For a couple of months, he had a stint on TBS, during the period when McMahon's national expansion had failed to replace the old Georgia show on Turner's Atlanta-based cable station. The morning viewing of Mid South did so well compared to the canned WWF programing and the retread of Ole Anderson's Georgia revival, that Turner infamously gave Watts a handshake agreement to take over the historic Saturday night 6:05 p.m. show. Instead, Turner went behind Watts's back and brokered a deal to have McMahon sell the time slot to Crockett.

By the time Watts tried to go national in 1986, he had already lost. His Universal Wrestling Federation had exciting television and great ratings, but by paying for time-slot clearances, Watts was bleeding money. For the first time in his career as a promoter, the strong television ratings weren't producing strong ticket sales. The national campaign floundered. His out-of-territory house shows were a disaster, and the ones in the territory were struggling because of the economy. In 1987, Watts sold the UWF to Crockett, who, in addition to getting the TBS spot, was now the last of the old-guard NWA promoters. Crockett had gone national successfully, at least in the short term. He promised Watts $4 million for the UWF, but his booker, Dusty Rhodes, in a fit of ego, destroyed most of the assets within a matter of months. McMahon had famously, in wrestling legend if not in reality, told Crockett that he would choke on the million dollars he paid for the TBS show. As it turned out, Crockett choked on the million or so dollars he paid (he never paid the rest of the $4 million) for the UWF assets. Crockett ended up selling his promotion to Ted Turner, and everyone knows how poorly that ended. Or, for that matter, began.

Watts didn't just have the one Last Stampede, either. Perhaps asking a wrestler to have one retirement, or just one comeback, is like asking an alcoholic to have just one drink. In 1985, when his protégé, Jim Duggan, got burned by the evil Skandar Akbar's fireball, Watts came back to get revenge, calling it, The Stampede's Alive in '85. Watts copied the JYD blinding with Duggan losing his eyesight, and then, when Duggan returned, he copied the old Stagger Lee idea, too. Wrestling with Duggan against Akbar's monster heel tag team of Kamala and Kareem Muhammad (Ray Candy, now even fatter at over 400 pounds), Watts suffered a surprise defeat in a loser-leaves-town match. He returned as the Midnight Rider.

In all, Watts brought back all three of his biggest angles that summer: the blinding, the masked man, and the Stampede. However, none of them worked like they had first time. Business was okay, but only just. Unfortunately, it wasn't the final Last Stampede, either.

The next summer, with the UWF start-up struggling, Watts pulled the hated Russians gimmick out of mothballs and was attacked by Korchenko. Crockett gave the UWF the Koloffs on loan for six-man tags against Watts, Steve "Dr. Death" Williams, and Hacksaw Duggan. Watts gained his revenge, but not box office success. The television angle was super heated, with Jim Ross selling the draping of the Russian flag over Watts as if the Cowboy had been murdered in cold blood. It was super heat . . . except it didn't work. The angle didn't draw.

As Watts's partner in Houston, the late Paul Boesch, told Dave Meltzer in the *Wrestling Observer Newsletter*, "the first time Watts came out of retirement, it was pure genius. The second time they did the angle, it was okay. The third time, nobody wanted to see it."

Watts's real last stampede came on June 14, 1986, at the 'Dome.

He teamed with Rhodes and Williams and beat the Russians in a six-man "street fight." The match was loaded with the stars of the UWF and the NWA. DiBiase fought Hayes. Terry Taylor feuded with Buzz Sawyer. The Fantastics fought the Sheepherders. Despite the hot Russian angle and the loaded card, it drew only 7,200 fans and a gate of $70,000. In the co-main event, Ric Flair defended the world title against Ricky Morton. After the show, Watts told Meltzer that the title match had been the problem. "Everyone loves Ricky Morton, but no one here believed he could possibly beat Ric Flair." Morton and Flair were feuding on Crockett's television program. A few weeks after the Superdome show, they drew 25,000 fans to Crockett's old territorial home base of Charlotte for a stadium show. Clearly, some fans believed he could win.

As soon as Watts's feud with the Russians wrapped, one with the Freebirds began. It literally happened in the same match. After Watts squashed Korchenko in the blowoff, the Freebirds attacked Watts to shift into another summer Stampede. Then they attacked his new protégé, Williams, and "broke" his arm. Once again, Watts swore revenge. As with the Russians, it looked good on television, but bombed at the box office. This feud didn't even make it to the 'Dome. By the time the traditional November show rolled around, the booking had aready shifted to new rivalries.

Watts finally wrestled his last match in the summer of 1986. The UWF died for good, at the hands of Rhodes's booking, at the 1987 Thanksgiving show. By then, of course, the Junkyard Dog was long gone. In Watts's mind, however, he was never forgotten. Mid South, the UWF, and even Turner's renamed World Championship Wrestling tried again and again to remake the Junkyard Dog. In the end, they even tried to do it with the Junkyard Dog himself.

CHAPTER EIGHT

OFTEN IMITATED . . .

Like many professional wrestlers, George Wells came to the sport from football. Unlike others, he had a decent amount of gridiron success, starting as a defensive lineman at New Mexico State and playing for nearly a decade in Canada. While he didn't make it to the NFL, he was an all-star for Hamilton and Saskatchewan, and played in three Grey Cups, winning one. Like Ernie Ladd before him, he started wrestling in the off-season, and when he eventually retired from football he stepped into the ring full time. He had early success, too, holding the prestigious United States title in his native San Francisco, and then making the rounds to the other territories. About the time he got to Mid South in 1984, things started going bad.

When the Junkyard Dog left Mid South for the World Wrestling Federation, Bill Watts called in Wells as a replacement. Wells had the athletic background Watts liked, and of course, he was black. He wasn't much of a worker, but since it hadn't mattered with JYD, Watts figured it wouldn't matter with Wells. He dubbed him "Master Gee" George Wells, gave him a popular break dancing–era theme song, and proceeded to put him over every bad guy in the territory in quick squashes, just as he had done with JYD. Right away on television, Wells beat JYD's chief rival, "Hacksaw" Butch Reed, so quickly and so decisively that it should have killed Reed altogether. "Junkyard Dog never beat Butch Reed like that," Watts reminded his audience at every opportunity, quickly adding that the pressure from Reed had made JYD "crack" and leave for easier competition.

Watts believed it was a foolproof plan: he'd replace the Junkyard Dog and make a new star at the same time. However, it worked so poorly, so many different times, with so many different guys replacing JYD, that you might wonder who the fool was. As the cliché goes, imitation is the sincerest form of flattery. By that logic, Bill Watts spent the rest of his time in wrestling flattering the Junkyard Dog. He tried so many times in Mid South over a two-year period that he resembled an addict. But Watts wasn't chasing a high. He was chasing a segment of his audience that he lost when JYD went down to Mr. Wrestling II and then skipped town for the WWF. Undaunted, Watts tried again in his national expansion, the UWF. However, the crowds that loved JYD weren't fooled into thinking a random black man could be a superstar simply because of his skin color. Watts tried one last time during his dismal run at the helm of Ted Turner's World Championship Wrestling, going so far as to break the color barrier on the world championship. That program ended in disappointment, as well.

Wrestling had such a long and successful history with ethnic baby-faces that it probably never occurred to Watts that he had caught lightning in a bottle with JYD. Promoters and bookers make stars. That's their job — they make stars and program them in angles and matches that make money. So, of course Watts and his various bookers thought they could do it again. Whenever Dick Murdoch stormed out on him, Watts replaced him. When talent jumped from his small pond to the big oceans of Crockett or McMahon, Watts replaced them. It stood to reason that Watts, one of the better promoters in the wrestling business, could take another black wrestler and push him in a way that brought the black crowds back to the arena. But he never could.

Wells didn't last long. What he lacked was the thing that made the Junkyard Dog successful: charisma. Worse, the other thing he had in common with JYD was a cocaine problem. He was unreliable out of the ring and unremarkable in it. Within months, the outcome was clear. Actually, to those on the inside, it was obvious within weeks.

By the end of the year, Wells had followed JYD to the WWF. If Mid South had not been done with him already, it would have been one of the talent hirings that could have been labelled as a predatory business practice on the part of the WWF. Wells had even less success in the WWF than Mr. Wrestling II. At least in Mid South he had a push up the ladder. In the WWF, he came in as a preliminary wrestler and pretty much stayed there. When the WWF tried to run competition to Mid South in Watts's cities, it often brought in JYD to headline the shows. On those same cards, Wells worked opening matches and lost. He did stay on the roster for a couple of years. In 1986, at WrestleMania II, he got a moment of glory, or at least infamy, when he lost to Jake "The Snake" Roberts. With Wells "knocked out" from Roberts's killer DDT, Roberts pulled his pet python, Damien, out of a bag and wrapped it around his fallen opponent. He stuck the snake's head in Wells's face as the announcers screamed their disgust. At least Wells's story ended more positively than

JYD's outside the ring; he cleaned up his life, and now works to keep inner city kids off of drugs in his native northern California.

Back in Mid South, the territory was on such a hot streak in 1984 that the failure to replace JYD hardly mattered. The teens were coming for the good-looking, young babyfaces, the hard-core fans were coming for the solid booking and exciting matches, and the television ratings and gates were great. Unfortunately for Watts, he didn't learn his lesson with Wells. He simply thought he had picked the wrong guy to replace the Junkyard Dog.

In late 1984, Watts decided to try again. This time he chose a familiar name, JYD's former rival, "Hacksaw" Butch Reed. Reed had been missing in action after he had been destroyed by Wells. While he was gone, "General" Skandar Akbar had made his return to Mid South, and as he had in 1983 under similar circumstances, began acquiring an "army." The previous go-round, Akbar formed a relationship with Ted DiBiase and co-opted the Rat Pack. This time, Akbar took over for Jim Cornette, even acquiring his bodyguard, Hercules Hernandez. Then Akbar renewed his relationship with DiBiase and started up one with "Doctor Death" Steve Williams. Then he brought back Kamala the Ugandan Giant. Finally, he started making overtures to Reed's tag team partner, "Nature Boy" Buddy Landel.

In one of the typical episodic segments that Mid South built and ran so well on television, Akbar curried favor with Landel. First he gave him a gold watch, which Landel put on his wrist. A week later, when Landel was still wearing the gold watch, Akbar scolded, "You know what that watch is for." When Reed finally showed up, he demanded to know what Landel was doing with Akbar. Jim Duggan had done the exact same thing when Ted DiBiase began associating with the hated "Arab," only this time Landel had a gold watch. He offered it to Reed. He told him that the watch was only the beginning. Reed took the watch, held it up to the crowd and announced, "So this is what the watch is for!" Then he threw the watch down and stomped on it. The "army" then attacked Reed. Of course, he fought off Landel and got some licks in on the others, but Kamala eventually laid him out. His old rival, Duggan, the other "Hacksaw," made the save. It's worth noting the mistake Watts made right off the bat; no one ever had to make the save for the Junkyard Dog. It certainly wouldn't be the last mistake made in Reed's face turn.

On the November Superdome Spectacular, Reed and Duggan teamed up in the third match of a five-match card. They beat DiBiase and Williams. The co-main events were the Rock 'n' Roll Express beating the Midnight Express in the feud-ending, blowoff "scaffold" match, and Magnum T.A. beating Ernie Ladd by disqualification while trying to regain the North American title. Master Gee teamed with "Brickhouse" Brown, another black wrestler who was not catching fire in Mid South, in the opening match. They were squashed by Hector and Chavo Guerrero. The card drew 7,500 fans, about a third of what the two summer shows had drawn. Already, there were doubts about Reed.

Unlike Wells and some of the more unbelievable copycat attempts later, Butch Reed had a chance to get over. While his failure to catch fire became the subject of much speculation, the biggest problem was in the booking. He had charisma, a muscular build, good power moves, good working ability, and gave a decent interview. What he never got was the JYD treatment. Of course, he had spent years losing to JYD and had spent the summer of 1984 putting over Wells. In theory, face turns erased previous losses. Still, there was no superhero push. Reed did gain some revenge on Landel, but as 1985 began, he found himself struggling to beat DiBiase, Williams, and Hernandez. He came out a definitive loser in the feud against Kamala. By the spring, he was also losing his feud, and his specialty match, the Ghetto Street Fight, to newcomer Nord the Barbarian.

At the same time, the North American title was floating around looking for a champion. Magnum T.A. lost the belt to Ladd in October 1984. Ladd, on his last legs, or at least failing knees, kept the title for only two months before losing it and retiring soon after. He dropped the strap in December, not to Reed, but to Brad Armstrong, a small, second-generation wrestler who had good success in Georgia, but no box office juice in Mid South. Armstrong held the title for only six weeks before dropping it to DiBiase in January 1985. By March, DiBiase had dropped the title to Terry Taylor, who was being pushed from a position as a semi–main event babyface into a headliner. The ultimate goal was to have him challenge Ric Flair for the world title.

The type of superhero JYD push Reed needed went, instead, to Taylor. By no means was the future Red Rooster a bad wrestler. On the contrary, he was a good worker. He was the type of wrestler, as Mick Foley would joke about a decade later, that every federation needed. "Lightweight babyface keeps on kicking out," Foley, a.k.a. Cactus Jack, joked in one memorable interview. Taylor had been a solid part of the package during the 1984 success, drawing the young girls, and therefore the young guys who followed the young girls, into the crowd. Taylor certainly didn't need a superhero push to draw girls; he was a chick magnet. He needed to get beat on, bleed, make the girls screech for him, and make against-all-odds kick-outs and comebacks. Even when he sometimes lost, the girls felt bad for him and kept supporting him. He wasn't going to draw hard-core fans, and he certainly wasn't going to lure the black audience back to the matches. Reed might have, given the right push or angle. Unfortunately, the promotion blew his turn and then wondered why it didn't work. Inside the office, they blamed Reed rather than themselves.

On March 30, 1985, at the 'Dome, Duggan and DiBiase brought the climax to their hot feud to New Orleans. Based on a unique angle about who was the better dressed man, the stylish DiBiase or the goofy, redneck Duggan — the fans, of course, picked Duggan — the payoff matches were bringing some relief to the sagging business. The blowoff was a "loser leaves town, coal miner's glove, steel cage, tuxedo death match." Although it had sold out several shows around the territory, it drew 9,500 fans and a $100,000 gate to the 'Dome. About halfway through the card, Nord beat Reed in a Ghetto Street Fight. Not long after that, Reed left for the AWA, but he was back sooner than anyone expected. Ultimately, Watts deemed Taylor's push a failure, but Taylor, too, would get another shot soon enough.

Reed wasn't even out the door when another attempt to replace JYD began. Before Taylor won the North American title, he had been booked to regain the television title. When he moved up to the main belt, the television title was put up for grabs in a tournament held over several months at the television tapings. "Hacksaw" Duggan looked to be the favorite, but he was injured by Akbar's henchmen in the infamous fireball angle. Heroically taking Duggan's place was a wrestler known only as the Snowman.

Eddie Crawford had no history in wrestling. In some ways, aside from the fact that he was black, he resembled the Junkyard Dog. He was a good talker. He had some charisma, although not as much as JYD. He couldn't work at all — at least he had that going for him. He was unknown in the wrestling world; perhaps Watts thought he was making JYD over from scratch. Indeed, he got the superhero push that Reed had lacked. The Snowman entered the television title tournament while it was already underway, taking Duggan's place in the third round. He squashed Williams in the semi-finals, and then Jake Roberts in the finals to win the medal that Watts used instead of a title belt.

The Snowman won the title in May 1985. For the Superdome show in June, Watts and his assistant, Jim Ross, came up with a plan to "make" the Snowman. They billed him as a former boxer, the protégé of Muhammad Ali. They pushed a rematch with Snowman and Roberts in which Snowman would have Ali in his corner. Ali had worked the debut

WrestleMania that spring, and agreed to come in for the Superdome show. However, his Parkinson's disease was affecting his charisma and his famous ability to give an incredible interview. His promos, in which he proclaimed his support for his protégé, were unconvincing. As Dave Meltzer put it in his newsletter, Ali sounded like he had no clue who his protégé was. As if that wasn't problematic enough, the heels in the dressing room were revolting. They hated Crawford, and hated getting squashed by him. Roberts began making noise about not doing business for him. Despite all this, Watts and Ross believed they were remaking the Junkyard Dog. With the economy ailing, they dropped general admission tickets to $5. Privately, they talked about having their first Superdome card with a legit crowd of 30,000 plus.

The June 1, 1985, Superdome show ended up drawing 11,000 fans. While the attendance was up from the past two shows, it was much lower than the record levels of 1980 to 1984, and clearly way below the 30,000 mark. Worse, because ticket prices had been scaled back, the gate was just $98,000, slightly lower than the March show, with fewer fans in attendance. The Snowman versus Jake Roberts match went midway through the event, with four matches after it. Roberts, angry at the booking, pulled a Dick Murdoch. He had a stinker of a match, refusing to work with Crawford. When they got to the part when Ali was supposed to deck Roberts, Roberts refused to sell the punch. Somehow, Watts managed to not deck Roberts himself, but he was furious. In the other top matches, Flair successfully defended his world title against Taylor, ending Taylor's skyward push. WWF cast-off Sgt. Slaughter made a special appearance with his protégé, Terry Daniels, and beat the Dirty White Boys. DiBiase and Williams beat the Rock 'n' Roll Express, and Duggan beat Kamala.

Another 'Dome show was booked for August. There were various ideas about where the booking should go, but one idea was certain. The Snowman was going nowhere. A month later, he dropped the television title to "Dirty" Dutch Mantel. Mantel was just a transitional champion. He held the medal for two weeks before dropping it to Butch Reed. Reed had been wasted in the AWA, and was brought back to fill the void left by the Snowman. He quickly won the television title, and in August his superhero push finally began as he moved into the role of world title challenger against Flair. The August 10, 1985, 'Dome show was the best-attended show of the final three years of the business, but it was only a modest success. It did draw 15,800 fans, but ticket prices were lowered again, so the gate was just $107,000. Kamala and Kareem Muhammad beat Duggan and Watts in the loser-leaves-town match as a co-main event. Reed, of course, didn't win the world title, but he was pushed strongly in losing.

In the fall, Reed won the North American title from Dick Murdoch. Business was okay, but nowhere near the level of the top of the Junkyard Dog era. JYD's fan base never truly embraced Reed, but in retrospect, that's just part of wrestling. Fans have their interests peaked, they get hot for the action, and when it cools they lose interest. The secret to sustained business is to make new fans, build new stars, new issues. For Watts, who was trying to squeeze big crowds out of small markets, the problem was bigger than Butch Reed. It was about the economy and the changes in the business of wrestling. The territory system was all but dead. The Watts business model would soon die, as well.

Reed lasted through the end of the year, but he, too, got eaten up by personal problems. His marriage was falling apart — his wife was in Missouri, not in the middle of the territory where most of the workers set up their home base. The seven-day-a-week grind of Mid South's schedule was getting to him, and her. The money wasn't what it used to be, either, and that made everyone tense. To top it off, Reed, too, started having problems with cocaine. His wife confronted Watts, who says he responded, "I'm not the one sticking all that powder up his nose."

Finally, she gave Reed an ultimatum. He dropped the title to Dick

Slater on New Year's Day 1986 and was gone from Mid South for good. His career largely fell off from there. He had a brief WWF run, working with bleached-blond hair as "the Natural" Butch Reed, and appeared in WrestleMania IV, losing a tournament match to Randy Savage. Later, he turned up in WCW as part of the Doom tag team with Ron Simmons. At first they were masked men, mostly going under to the Road Warriors and the Steiners. Once unmasked, they had a successful run as WCW champs. But it was Simmons who got the star turn, and Reed was cast off. He returned for Bill Watts when Watts took over WCW, but was fired when he failed to show up for a television taping.

Later in 1986, when Mid South became the UWF, Watts tried to replace the Junkyard Dog again. Eddie Sharkey, a trainer renowned for finding big muscle-headed gym rats and turning them into power-house wrestlers, had a guy with some potential. He was slightly older for a guy breaking into wrestling, very green, but he had a good look. He had gotten his feet wet in Winnipeg, one of Verne Gagne's old cities. Sharkey had trained the Road Warriors, Nikita Koloff, Rick Rude, and Krusher Krushchev, so he had a good track record. Watts decided to take a look at the guy, whose real name was Ted Russell. He renamed him Savannah Jack, and he got a push, beating Buddy Roberts for the UWF television title on November 9, 1986. He held the title for five months before losing it to Eddie Gilbert in the waning days of Watts's involvement with the promotion. With the sale to Crockett being negotiated, the UWF held the Superblast at the Superdome show on April 11, 1987. In a semi-main event, Jack beat "Iceman" King Parsons in a Ghetto Street Fight. Williams challenged One Man Gang, and the Freebirds fought Skandar Akbar's army in the co-main events. The show drew just 3,000 fans. Jack didn't catch on with Crockett, and like most of those who didn't, went to work Texas indies. As with many of the workers in the steroid era, his body gave out, and his career ended with a series of strokes and heart attacks. He returned to his native

Minnesota, and died at the beginning of 2012. In a 2011 article in his local newspaper, he proved that while he didn't have it in the ring, he did have a wrestler's ability to work in one respect: the article quotes him as saying his salary from Watts was $5,000 a week, and that he had wrestled in front of 60,000 fans at the Superdome.

In 1992, wrestling fans cheered when Bill Watts took over WCW. Their memories of the glory days, with Mid South and the UWF had been stoked by an interview with Watts in the *Pro Wrestling Torch* newsletter. Their desire to watch good wrestling had been abused weekly by the twin disasters of WCW under Jim Herd and an extreme low period in the WWF. Other than the hot indie scene at the time and a few brief highlights from a con-job by Joe Pedicino called Global Wrestling, there was nothing good about wrestling. The Cowboy rode into WCW as a savior. What happened next could be studied for years without producing much in the way of a satisfying explanation.

Watts admittedly had not watched wrestling since he had left it behind in 1987. He didn't know that Dusty Rhodes and Ole Anderson had been total failures in WCW, and were hated by the hard-core fans who were the only ones left watching. So, Watts saw nothing wrong with hiring his old friends to give it another go. Watts had not seen the innovations in wrestling, like high-flying top-rope maneuvers and the light-heavyweight division. So, he thought he was using smart booking when he banned moves from the top rope to get heat on them. He went back to the tried-and-true heavyweights that he had always successfully promoted and phased out the light-heavyweight division. He tried to cut salaries and save money; he actually did this so successfully that he alienated almost all of the well-paid athletes in his dressing room. He debuted his son Erik, and pushed him to the moon; he squashed all the fans' favorites. He struggled in the corporate culture, and failed to gain any traction in getting WCW accepted in the greater scheme of Turner Broadcasting. Worst of all, his big shows were almost universally horrible. Even his biggest fans were disappointed. He lasted less than a year, and wound up quitting just before he was to be fired.

Almost immediately after he was hired, Watts took up his pet project, making another Junkyard Dog. This time he picked Ron Simmons. To his credit, Simmons was a much better choice than George Wells, Eddie Crawford, or Ted Russell. But he was still no Sylvester Ritter. He wasn't even a Bruce Reed. Simmons had been a huge football star at Florida State, playing nose tackle from 1977 to 1980. He was a two-time all-American, and finished ninth in Heisman Trophy voting in 1979, a rare accomplishment for a defensive player. His number 50 was retired at FSU, one of only three jerseys that had been retired up to that point. He was drafted by the Cleveland Browns, played in the United States Football League (USFL) for the Tampa Bay Bandits, and in the Canadian Football League for the Ottawa Rough Riders.

In 1986, Simmons started wrestling. He was trained in Florida by Hiro Matsuda, who had also trained Paul Orndorff and Hulk Hogan. He got an immediate push in the dying days of the Florida territory because of his local ties and his credibility as a football player. When Crockett acquired the remnants of the old territory, Simmons went along, but he got lost in the shuffle. His Florida co-worker, Lex Lugar, another former USFL guy, got the super push and became a star immediately. Simmons teamed with Steve Williams, Watts's big star from the UWF, in a pairing of college standouts. They had one other thing in common: they were both being overlooked in the mergers. Williams had Japan to fall back on, and he became a much bigger star overseas than he ever did in the United States. Simmons went back to Florida for a spell, and floated around the new indie circuit.

In 1989, Simmons came back to WCW as part of the masked heel team, Doom. Originally, they were mere props for their manager, Woman, a.k.a. Nancy Sullivan, and later, Nancy Benoit. They were also mostly foils for the Steiner Brothers, Woman's main enemies. They lost up and down the circuit to the Steiners, as well as to most of the other babyface teams. At the traditional November pay-per-view Starrcade, the booking called for a round-robin tournament with four tag teams facing one another: Doom, the Steiners, the Road Warriors, and the Samoan Swat Team. Doom lost all three of its matches and finished last.

Their fortunes changed in 1990. They were unmasked, acknowledged their true identities, and got a new manager, Teddy Long. On May 19, 1990, in the semi-final match of the Capital Combat pay-per-view in Washington, D.C., Doom won the NWA tag team titles from the Steiners, and held them for the rest of the year. When Ted Turner's organization had a falling out with the NWA, they were the first team to be recognized as WCW champions. They lost the titles in February 1991 to the Freebirds, who by this point consisted of Michael Hayes and Jimmy Garvin. Simmons turned babyface soon after, and he feuded with Reed. The promotion wanted to push Simmons as a hero, and he went over Reed up and down the line. At the first Superbrawl, in May 1991 in St. Petersburg, Simmons decisively beat Reed in a steel cage match to win their feud. Unfortunately for him, WCW was a complete mess at this point. It was the summer of Ric Flair's firing — the chants of "we want Flair" filled arenas — and the dreaded booking committees that were making matches to stroke egos rather than generate business. Simmons was lost in the chaos.

Enter Bill Watts and his recurring desire to remake JYD. Simmons's football background and tough-guy appearance made him a perfect fit for the Cowboy. By mid-summer 1992, Watts was ready to push Simmons into a top spot. The WCW champion had been Vader, a 400-pound wrestler with revolutionary skills for someone his size. Sting, who got his first big push under Watts, had traded title reigns with Vader, and been the top star and leading contender. Watts saw Sting as a gimmick wrestler who didn't need a title to get over. So he planned a swerve.

Watts scheduled a match between Vader and Sting on August 2,

1992, in Baltimore, a town that had been in WWF territory, and had been one of the few success stories in the rivalry between WCW and the WWF. Jake Roberts attacked Sting and took him out of the match. Watts gave an interview in which he declared that a "random" drawing would determine who would get the title shot. Simmons's name was drawn. In the crowd were hundreds of fans who read the wrestling newsletters and considered themselves "smart" to the business. They were buzzing about what they expected to happen, and they were correct. Simmons won the title. It wasn't exactly true that there had never been a black world heavyweight champion. As far back as the '50s, Bobo Brazil and Art Thomas had held titles that were billed as world titles. More recently, "Iceman" King Parsons had held the belt in Dallas that Fritz Von Erich dubbed the world heavyweight title after he broke away from the NWA. However, in the lineage of the world titles of the three main territories, WWF, AWA, and NWA/WCW, it was, indeed, a history-making event. The fans, still popping for the idea of watching history being made gave Simmons and the match a huge ovation.

Unfortunately, that was the high point. As Watts himself later admitted, the new champ simply lacked something. He had fire, was a decent worker, and was okay on interviews, but perhaps he wasn't great at any one thing. Certainly, his challengers and feuds were lacking. Cactus Jack, the Barbarian, and later, Steve Williams got the bulk of the title shots. None of them were built up into title contenders. None of the angles popped. Reed came in for an ex-partners' feud that might have worked. Instead, he was fired before he had a chance. Whatever it was, having Simmons as champ just didn't work. Sting was still the top star and Simmons as champ didn't help business. Simmons faced Williams at Starrcade '92, in a match that ended in disqualification. He lost the title back to Vader a few days later. The experiment to remake JYD had failed again.

Ironically, for a guy who featured black athletes more often, and in a more positive light than most promoters, race played a role in Watts's downfall. The interview with *Pro Wrestling Torch*, which had won over the diehards and gotten the attention of the Turner execs, also turned out to be the beginning of the end of Watts's WCW tenure. At least it sort of led to it, or would have, had Watts not decided to resign before the controversy flared. In one part of the interview with *Torch* publisher Wade Keller, Watts went on a rant about Lester Maddox, the civil-rights-era villain who refused to serve black people at his restaurant in Georgia. In a fit of what might charitably be called his libertarian viewpoint, Watts stated that he believed Maddox had a right, as the owner of the business, to serve or not serve whoever he wanted. Watts's bosses had read the interview before they hired him — at least they gave every indication they had. However, one important Turner executive, the civil-rights and baseball icon Hank Aaron, had not. At least he hadn't read it until *Torch* columnist Mark Madden, a self-promoter of pro wrestling proportions who had gotten into a pissing match with Watts, faxed Aaron the original interview to get his comments. Watts felt like he had been misled in terms of the support he had within the company, and also in his ability to get Ted Turner's attention, and decided to quit. Had he not quit, it is very likely he would have been fired that day. Either way, neither he nor WCW nor Madden came out of the event looking good.

Toward the end of his WCW stint, Watts had an idea for making a new JYD. He called up Sylvester Ritter and asked him if he was interested in coming to WCW. Ritter had been bouncing around the indies using his name and what was left of his reputation to garner whatever payoff he could. He indicated that he was interested. When Watts tried to pursue it, he realized that JYD was in no condition, physically or mentally, to headline. Once and for all, Watts let it go. Neither man was a major factor in professional wrestling again.

CHAPTER NINE

BIG-TIME DECLINE

The Junkyard Dog certainly didn't walk into a bad situation after he left Mid South. In 1984, the year he arrived, the WWF had begun to revolutionize pro wrestling. Vincent Kennedy McMahon, a third generation promoter, had taken his father's territory and had begun to turn it into the first — some would say only — successful national wrestling company.

Vince McMahon Sr. ran Capitol Wrestling Corp., better known as the World Wide Wrestling Federation. He had one of the best territories in the business, the Northeast, or as it was known in wrestling shorthand,

New York. McMahon also had all of New England, including Boston, plus Philadelphia, New Jersey, and Baltimore. He ran Washington, D.C., where he had set up shop, as a city-state territory akin to Paul Boesch's Houston territory. He also had a working agreement with the Pittsburgh promotion, in no small part because McMahon's top star, Italian strongman Bruno Sammartino, lived there. He had so many advantages in promoting, including cities with large populations, the relatively short distances between his big towns, and the major media congregated in the Northeast. So much was in his favor that he largely pulled out of the monopolistic National Wrestling Alliance in the early '60s and ran the WWWF on its own, promoting Sammartino as the world champ. Later, he quietly rejoined the NWA and gave lip service to its world title, but he never promoted it. He did, however, maintain deep friendships and working relationships with the old guard of the NWA, particularly Eddie Graham in Florida and Sam Muchnick in St. Louis.

Business was so good, and the crowds so conditioned to attend house shows to see big matches, that WWWF and later WWF television rarely gave much away for free. WWWF television programs consisted of five or six squash matches in which wrestlers being pushed beat the same group of jobbers, or enhancement guys, over and over. Interviews, localized by market, and the occasional big angle or title change were all the promotion needed to draw big television audiences. Business was usually good. When the local hero, usually Bruno, but sometimes an ethnic babyface, like Puerto Rican Pedro Morales in New York and Philadelphia or Bobo Brazil in Washington, had a hot challenger, business was great. Because of these advantages, McMahon usually had his pick of talent. He also promoted national attraction Andre the Giant, and sent him all over the country to keep the gimmick from getting stale. Often, he sent Andre to territories as a peace offering right after he had hired away one of their local stars. In the

territorial era, going to New York from, say, Oklahoma or Kansas City was like being called up to the major leagues.

Bill Watts himself worked for McMahon in the '60s. He had been wrestling for McGuirk when Red Berry came in for a show in Wichita Falls. Berry teamed with Watts and was impressed, so he went back and told Vince Sr. and his partner at the time, "Toots" Mondt. They brought Watts in almost immediately. "That's where I first became 'Cowboy' Bill Watts," he said. "They told me, 'Well, you're from Oklahoma, so you're a cowboy.'" Watts had never been a cowboy, in the ring or out, but he went along with the gimmick and bought himself a cowboy hat in New Jersey. Watts originally worked New York as a babyface underneath Sammartino, setting up challengers for their main events and occasionally working as the champ's tag partner. Eventually, he turned on Sammartino and had a successful main-event heel run. After the run played itself out, he turned face again to set up the next series of challengers for Sammartino. Altogether, he stayed nearly two years, and didn't leave until late in 1965.

"I learned a lot there," Watts wrote, "including what not to do for TV presentation. I never liked the formula of star versus job guy for the whole show. I always thought the Northeast was the jewel of the industry *despite* the way matches were promoted, not because of it."

In the early '80s, Vince Jr. bought the promotion from his father and began to change the formula. Initially, his concern wasn't the television format; it was the territorial system itself. He got his product on cable television, much as the Georgia promotion had, but unlike his southern counterpart, he planned to use the platform to go national. First, he lucked into a slot on the USA Network when the station had issues with San Antonio's Southwest Championship Wrestling, run by Joe Blanchard. Then McMahon pulled a coup; he bought out several stock holders and took the WTBS time slot away from Georgia's Championship Wrestling. Although the WWF was expected, and had promised, to tape matches in the WTBS studio, it never did. Instead, they showed tape from their other shows, as well as highlights from rival promotions. At first, and to be honest, for a long time afterward, the rival promoters didn't take Vince Jr. seriously. They had a whole list of reasons why he would fail, including a bunch of wrestling truisms. As for showing their wrestlers on WTBS, they honestly felt he was giving them free advertising. It never occurred to them that he was showing highlights of the wrestlers he would sign away.

In late 1983, headliners from across the country began to disappear.

Some failed to show up at their scheduled dates, but many more simply gave notice and left without tipping their hands about their future plans. Either way, only the most insightful or most paranoid understood the huge change afoot. With his father's blessings, McMahon went national. In January 1984, he held a television taping in St. Louis, home of Muchnick, who had retired after being president of the NWA for many years. The show debuted much of the talent McMahon had squirreled away. Included in his new group of headliners was Hulk Hogan, the bleached-blond, orange-tanned superhero who would become one the biggest stars in wrestling history. Hogan had been a heel for the WWWF in 1980, feuding with Andre the Giant and Tony Atlas, among others. His feud with Andre went around the country, and even made it to the Superdome Spectacular on the famous show in 1980. More recently, he had been a headliner for Verne Gagne in the AWA — until he, too, disappeared. He was one of the wrestlers who left a slew of no-shows in his wake. Within weeks of his debut, Hogan became the WWF champion, a crown he would hold for the next four years. The shockwaves from the St. Louis taping were felt throughout the business: McMahon had gone into someone else's city, used everyone else's wrestlers, and declared war on the old system. Many of the old guard would never be able to absorb the shock. Even those who did, like Crockett, Watts, and Fritz Von Erich, did so much too late, their reactions slowed by their faith in their own products and mastery of their markets.

Mid South was not an immediate McMahon target; Gagne and the AWA were. McMahon not only took the top wrestlers from the Minnesota giant, but also his top manager, Bobby Heenan, his announcers, and even some of his office staff. With cities like San Francisco, Denver, Chicago, parts of Canada, and his home base of Minneapolis, Gagne had the biggest territory and billed his title as a world title. Gagne tried fighting back, and even got national exposure on ESPN. It only seemed to fire up McMahon more. No sooner would

Gagne groom a new star than McMahon would take him away. Gagne's reputation for cheating headliners out of their fair share of gates didn't help matters. His former employees lined up in the early days to bad-mouth him on local promos. Early WWF expansion–era house shows went toward the AWA's base with regularity. Gagne tried to team up with Crockett, Watts, and other NWA promoters for a venture called Pro Wrestling USA to strike back at McMahon's biggest cities. As the joke went, when the group got together to plan their promotion, they couldn't even agree on what they should order for lunch. In retrospect,

Gagne held on much longer than he had any right to, but stubborn pride didn't make his battle successful.

By the summer of 1984, McMahon was making plans to challenge Mid South, as well. Taking JYD was his first step. He probably believed taking the headliner away would enable him to compete head-to-head in Mid South's cities in much the same way taking Hogan had given him the advantage in the AWA circuit. On that score, he miscalculated. The Mid South crowds were trained to like believable, fast-paced action. Their wrestlers were athletic superheroes and pretty-boy babyfaces. The heels were either super workers, depended on to carry the action, or huge monsters. Television featured main-event-caliber matches, not the WWF roster of six squash matches and a big interview or angle sprinkled in every few weeks. Although the WWF had star power and a national platform, in the Mid South territory it was considered a distant second best, even third best in the markets that also received Von Erich's Dallas show. The WWF bombed going head-to-head in Oklahoma City and Tulsa. Much as the NWA cartel used to do, Watts loaded up shows in opposition and ran big angles to sway the fans. On several occasions he ran free shows, or cut ticket prices to below his break-even point, just to stop the invaders. Although he put a stop to this practice quickly — it was financial suicide — he was successful in the short run. The WWF did not have the same success in Watts's territory that it had in Gagne's.

In the '80s, the WWF ran two or three arenas a night, dubbed A, B, and C shows. A shows usually featured Hogan. C shows were often charity events in high school gyms. These shows used low-level guys, and were designed to spread goodwill and name recognition. The B shows were often headlined by the secondary titles, the tag team belts, or the Intercontinental title, plus a local hero from the old territory. The Junkyard Dog headlined many of these "B-shows" in 1984 and 1985. He often challenged for the Intercontinental title held by Greg

Valentine, and occasionally took a partner and challenged for the tag belts, as well. These angles were developed on television. Based on this exposure, the feud with Valentine went around the country as a main event or co-main event match. In Houston in the summer of 1985, the Dog-Valentine match headlined the Astro Arena, the small annex space adjacent to the Astrodome. The WWF ran the show between the usual Mid South/Houston City Wrestling (Boesch's promotion) ventures at the Sam Houston Coliseum. The Houston City shows had the Mid South crew and programs, plus Ric Flair defending his NWA title against Magnum T. A., and then Wahoo McDaniel. The first show sold out, and the second nearly sold out. The WWF had JYD against Valentine and the U.S. Express (Barry Windham and Mike Rotundo) against the Iron Sheik and Nikolai Volkoff for the tag team titles. It didn't come close to selling out. Ironically, failed JYD replacement George Wells wrestled in the second match of the WWF Astro Arena show, jobbing for Big John Studd.

In New Orleans, the war was different. The Louisiana Sports Commission held that there could only be one licensee for professional wrestling and Watts held that license. Furthermore, the head of the commission, Emile Bruneau, was not only a longtime friend of Watts's, but his son, Peppi, was Mid South's attorney. According to Watts, the Bruneaus were a rarity in Louisiana politics — honest, trustworthy, and not out for a kickback. However, the longtime Governor of Louisiana, Edwin Edwards, was the more typical pol: he and his cronies insisted on getting their share of the take. When the WWF petitioned the athletic commission for its own license, Watts spoke up in favor of ending the old system. He felt he could handle the competition, but he was tired of the patronage. And, in fact, he did handle the competition.

Not long after WrestleMania, in the summer of 1985, the WWF got its Superdome date. They brought in JYD and teamed him with Hogan, portraying them as the two biggest stars in the WWF and therefore in all of wrestling. They drew 6,000 fans, or about 30 percent of what Flair and Butch Reed would draw that summer. The WWF would eventually gain a foothold in Houston, helped by the defection of Paul Boesch after Watts sold the UWF without telling him. For the most part, however, it never drew in the Mid South territory during the Hogan era.

To the rest of the country, the WWF was becoming the big time. In 1984, with the help of rocker Cyndi Lauper and her then boyfriend/manager David Wolff, the WWF and MTV put on a series of specials that brought wrestling into mainstream focus. Lauper had used wrestling manager "Captain" Lou Albano in her video for the song "Girls Just Wanna Have Fun." The ensuing angle played off the video, each taking credit for the other's success. It led to the Brawl to Settle it All, in which Albano managed women's champ the Fabulous Moolah and Lauper seconded up-and-coming Wendi Richter in her title win. It was a big hit, and it led to a second appearance, a mock award show in which Albano and Lauper settled their feud by giving each other awards. Alas, Roddy Piper protested and used one of the awards, a gimmicked gold record of Lauper's hit song, to clock Albano. Hulk Hogan saved the day, and he and Piper were set up for a showdown.

On February 18, 1985, based on the buzz created by what the WWF called the "Rock and Wrestling Connection," a third MTV special aired, this one for a live prime-time show called The War to Settle the Score. Although it's no longer the case, in the mid-'80s, MTV was the epitome of pop culture. Being talked about on MTV News or by the station's VJs gave the federation a cool that money couldn't buy and the Mid Souths and Central States of the world couldn't match. The New York media establishment took notice. A merchandising wave followed. Suddenly, wrestling wasn't rasslin'. It was well on its way to being McMahon's vision of sports entertainment. Wrestling action figures, foam fingers, Hulkamania T-shirts, ice cream bars, and even a Saturday morning cartoon show on CBS followed. The Junkyard Dog was one of the top characters on the cartoon, and one of the top wrestlers in the whole marketing scheme.

The War to Settle the Score ended indecisively, but it was the highest-rated program ever aired on MTV. The previous record was held by The Brawl to Settle it All. Like any good angle, the MTV special set up the big show. In this case, the big show was the first WrestleMania, on March 31, 1985. McMahon booked a show at Madison Square Garden that would be sent out nationwide on closed-circuit television — a format that had worked for boxing, and on a regional basis for Jim Crockett in wrestling. It was a huge gamble. In fact, the entire company may have been riding on the show's success. In the main event, Hogan teamed with television star Mr. T against Roddy Piper and Paul Orndorff. Underneath, JYD challenged Greg Valentine for the Intercontinental title. The media blitz that focused on Hogan and Mr. T was unprecedented. The duo even hosted *Saturday Night Live* the night before the big show. Ticket sales were weak, and the promotion was cancelling venues leading up to the match. They were afraid they wouldn't even cover the deposits on the venues. An incredible walk-up audience saved the day, and the show ended up grossing more than $4 million. WrestleMania is now the biggest annual event in wrestling.

JYD continued to be a big part of the mix. Soon, he had his own wrestling action figure, complete with a dog collar and chain. The WWF scored again with a show on NBC, called *Saturday Night's Main Event*, which would replace *Saturday Night Live* several times a year. The first one aired in May 1985, and had just four matches: a reprise of the WrestleMania feud with Hogan wrestling Piper's bodyguard, "Cowboy" Bob Orton; a six-man tag based around the tag team titles; a women's title rematch; and the Junkyard Dog beating jobber Pete Dougherty.

About the same time, the WWF released its first LP, *The Wrestling*

Album. The centerpiece was a cover of the song "Land of a Thousand Dances," written by Chris Kenner and most famously recorded by Wilson Pickett. In the WWF version, all of the top wrestlers sang a line or two of the song. A video got heavy play on MTV, and was repeated on all the WWF television programs. To the old-school promoters, it exposed the business as being fake, as it had the heels and babyfaces singing together — although they did brawl at the end of the video. The video, and the album itself, is best described as campy. A less generous review would call it corny, grating, or just plain bad. JYD had one of the featured songs, and it certainly straddled the line between camp and awful. It was called "Grab Them Cakes," and featured him in a duet with disco singer Vicki Sue Robinson. It can now be interpreted as a pre-rap double-entendre, a more subtle version of "I like big butts and I can not lie." Or, it may have just been an inside joke about JYD's expanding waistline. In retrospect, it may not have straddled a line — it may have fallen fully on the awful side. However, quality aside, the message was clear; in 1985, JYD was one of the biggest stars in the WWF.

Unfortunately, his personal problems only worsened. The WWF roster wasn't the most notorious drug-using locker room. That sad honor went to World Class, where David Von Erich had already died under mysterious circumstances, Gino Hernandez would overdose the next year, the Freebirds were busy digging Terry Gordy an early grave, and the Von Erich kids were making a mockery of their dad's efforts to promote his sons as perfect Christian warriors. However, the WWF certainly had its share of drugs. With the success of Hogan and the Road Warriors in Georgia, steroid-era muscle men had seemingly become universal. In the '90s, when McMahon and a Pennsylvania doctor fought an indictment that they were selling the drugs to McMahon's crew, one of the more amazing aspects of the case was the list of names who testified that they were on steroids. Hogan was obvious; but even the little guys, like Piper, Rick Martel, and Brian Blair, were using.

Recreational drug use occurred, as well. With three tours on the road nearly all the time, most of the roster was on month-long road trips, crisscrossing the country with no time at home, no time to recover from injuries, no time to do anything but travel, wrestle, and party. Cocaine was huge in the mid-'80s, and wrestling seemed to be on the cutting edge of coke and even crack use. Plus, uppers and downers were often used to get up for performances, settle down late at night, and then get up to travel again for the next show.

JYD had been a notorious user, even in his Mid South days. Now, he was making three or four times as much money, with most of it still going up his nose. His weight ballooned even further, to the point where he was probably closer to 400 pounds. In the fledgling newsletters, like Dave Meltzer's *Wrestling Observer Newsletter*, JYD became known as JFD, the Junk Food Dog. His act in the ring grew worse, too. In Mid South, Watts would disguise JYD's lack of working skills with guys like DiBiase, Reed, and the Midnight Express, who could create motion around him and go flying when he made his comebacks. Up and down the lineup Watts had good workers to put in long matches and athletic displays to make up for the short, awkward main events. The WWF went in the other direction. From the beginning of the Vince McMahon Jr. era, the matches were secondary to the spectacle. Hogan was no great worker, either. In fact, all his matches looked more or less the same, a fact exposed on a video release a couple of years later that showed two Hogan title defenses against Harley Race back to back. The matches had similar booking and exactly the same finishes. Perhaps heads rolled over the video mistake, or perhaps no one cared. Television matches were mere minutes, and the longer ones on NBC had prearranged commercial breaks where the action seemed to wane at just the right time. There was no one to sell that the "Junkyard Dog doesn't get paid by the hour" or that JYD was bulking up for bigger competition. In the WWF style of sports entertainment, no one needed to make such statements.

Along the way, JYD became a caricature, a sort of throwback to the way black babyface wrestlers were handled a decade or two earlier. His head-butt became a bigger move in his arsenal, dating back to the Bobo Brazil–era logic that blacks always have hard heads. It wasn't even the old-style standing or leaping head-butt; instead, JYD got down on all fours and crawled his way into the move. It might have exposed the business as being fake, if nearly everything on the WWF's television at that time had not been doing the same thing. In character, JYD became a snarling, barking caricature. His interviews, which used to be much more thoughtful, became dog-like, as well. He wasn't just a long way from the Mid South JYD; he was a long way from Sylvester Ritter, the political-science major with the quick wit and sharp tongue. Of course, in many ways, the descent was more personal than professional. While many factions would seize upon the racial aspect of the character change — something seen again a few years later when Tony Atlas came in for a third WWF run and went from being Mr. USA to being Saba Simba — it is worth noting that the character change and personal decline happened with plenty of white headliners, too. A few years later, "Hacksaw" Duggan jumped to the WWF and became an even bigger caricature than JYD, and almost as poor a worker, settling into the same substitute-Hogan headline act that JYD once filled. When Dusty Rhodes finally came in, they put him in yellow polka dots and turned his "son-of-a-plumber, American dream" schtick around on him, making him stick his hand into a toilet and jive, "doo-doo is good for me, and doo-doo is good for you."

As with many wrestlers, the road didn't just take its toll on JYD, it wrecked his home life. His daughter had gone to live with his family, because he was almost never home. His ex-wife had been committed, but according to Meltzer, in the middle of the big business run of 1985, she escaped and kidnapped her daughter from JYD's grandmother. "He immediately chartered a plane back home, went to her brother's house, and broke down the door," Meltzer wrote in JYD's obituary issue. "The brother, who was a local police officer, tried to stop him, and the two scrambled trying to be the first to get a gun, which went off, shooting the police officer in the side of his stomach. It was ruled an accidental shooting."

By comparison, the ring was a safe haven, and JYD's WWF push continued. In November 1985, the WWF held its first pay-per-view using the cable technology that would transform the sport. At the Rosemont Horizon, in a suburb of Chicago, they held the Wrestling Classic, a tournament to crown the king of the WWF. The tournament shared billing with a Hogan-Piper rematch. It drew limited buys, since the technology was in its infancy. At that point, a subscriber had to go to the cable company and purchase the event directly from them. In return, the cable company provided a descrambler that the customer attached between their television and cable box to view the event. The show drew enough interest to point the WWF in the direction of pay-per-view and away from the costly closed-circuit events. The Junkyard Dog won the tournament (and allegedly a car) by defeating the Iron Sheik, Moondog Spot, and Randy Savage, the latter by count-out.

WrestleMania II was a bigger success on pay-per-view, clearing 100,000 buys. Although the product was a bit of a comedown from the inaugural event, it set the stage for the game-changing show the next year. It was also replayed on Showtime, which was another feather in the cap of the WWF, although the partnership didn't endure. In an attempt to one-up Crockett's dual-location Starrcade the year before, the show was held in three cities, Los Angeles, New York, and Chicago. The Junkyard Dog had been feuding with Terry Funk at the time, and had lost several matches when Funk's brother Dory, called Hoss, and "brother" Jimmy Jack (a.k.a. Jessie Barr) got involved. In the Los Angeles portion of WrestleMania, JYD teamed with Tito Santana to gain revenge. They came up short, losing the match because the Funks cheated. However, Meltzer's *Wrestling Observer* called it the best match of the show. On the ensuing *Saturday Night's Main Event*, JYD teamed with Hogan and finally got his revenge on the Funks.

The next year, 1987, while Watts's old UWF was failing and about to be sold, and with Jim Crockett about to bankrupt his promotion for the sake of Dusty Rhodes's ego, McMahon and the WWF had their biggest success. WrestleMania III had been booked into the Pontiac Silverdome in Michigan, a venue that held 93,000 fans. It may be apocryphal, but McMahon allegedly booked the show after he noticed that the Pope had filled the Silverdome on his North American tour. Proclaiming that he was bigger than God, McMahon booked the site. To headline the show, he called his dad's touring attraction, Andre the Giant, out of retirement, turned him heel, and put on a P. T. Barnum–like act for the "never before seen" battle of the giants. Of course, Hogan and Andre had feuded all across the country in 1980, with Andre as the good guy and Hogan as the heel that went down to defeat, but that was just truth, not marketing.

WrestleMania III was, indeed, a spectacular. It didn't quite draw the 93,000 that was announced as the attendance, but it did draw a record 78,000 fans and a stunning $1.6 million gate. Another half million fans paid $19.95 each to watch it on pay-per-view. Although the money had unquestionably been drawn by the Hogan-Andre showdown, the match between Ricky Steamboat and Randy Savage stole the show. JYD wrestled midway through the evening, going down to Harley Race, the new king, in a match in which the loser had to bow before the winner. Although he lost, JYD bowed only halfheartedly, and then, to the delight of the fans, walloped Race and chased him from the ring.

Still, JYD's push was winding down. His drug use was out of control, and his matches were bad, even by WWF standards. He began to gain a reputation for missing shows — or showing up in no condition to wrestle. His appearances on the Saturday night showcase ended. His place at the top of the B-shows was taken by Duggan, his old Mid South running mate. His spots on pay-per-views sunk lower and lower. Amazingly, he held on for another year. At WrestleMania IV, the vacant WWF title would be won by Savage, who had entered the WWF at the same time as JYD, lost to him in the Wrestling Classic three years earlier, and whose star was still on the rise in 1988. Savage beat Butch Reed in an early match, and another of JYD's old running mates, Ted DiBiase, now the top heel as the Million Dollar Man, in the finals. JYD wasn't in the tournament. He simply wasn't one of the top dozen WWF stars anymore. He worked with the rest of the pack in an opening-card battle royal. He did eliminate Harley Race and lasted until the end of the match, but he was tossed by Bret Hart, the Calgary star who was on his way up, as well.

The Junkyard Dog wasn't just on his way down; he was on his way out. Not long after the big show, the WWF purged its roster in a sweeping cost-cutting move. Many big names of the past, such as Don Muraco and Ken Patera, were gone. Sadly, the Junkyard Dog fit that bill, as well. He was only 35 years old. He should have been hitting his peak as a headliner and enjoying another five to ten years on top. Instead, he was spent. "Addiction is horrible, and is no respecter of talent," Watts said. "It is a destroyer of it."

In 1989, WCW took a chance on JYD. Although the group's business was struggling, it had a decent second year under Ted Turner. Or at least it did once Ricky Steamboat made a surprise return, his first since he had left for the WWF nearly five years earlier. Steamboat was immediately programmed with Ric Flair for the world title and won it in short fashion, taking the championship at the Chi-Town Rumble pay-per-view on February 20, 1989. It would become the first of a three-match series between the two men, and the program became an instant classic. The second match was scheduled for the Superdome at the sixth version of Clash of the Champions, a TBS special on April 2, 1989, that ran opposite WrestleMania V.

With a huge block of tickets to sell — the company was having trouble in that regard — the booking committee decided that its New Orleans show needed a blast from the past. The Junkyard Dog got the call first. Butch Reed also worked for WCW at this point, so they booked JYD and Reed in an undercard feud. It was their first Superdome match against each other in five years. Unfortunately, JYD's problems were worse than ever. According to Dave Meltzer, JYD had missed eight shows prior to the Clash, and would have been fired had management not felt they needed him to sell tickets. They had also put together a pre-match video on the Junkyard Dog and the history of New Orleans wrestling that they didn't want to go to waste. The match was bad, the crowd didn't react at all, and no one cared when JYD rolled up Reed for the pin. The show drew horribly. A little more than 1,000 people actually paid for their tickets. The company tried to "paper" the show (or give away free tickets to fill seats), and still only managed a crowd of 5,300. The announcers claimed there were more than 25,000 people in attendance, although it was clear there weren't anywhere near that number. Ironically, Michael Hayes was doing color commentary for the event. Without gagging or laughing, he said, "I held the attendance record in this building, but that record may be in jeopardy with the tremendous crowd we have tonight."

As a side note, Steamboat did successfully defend the title against Flair in a 55-minute, three-fall match that is regarded as a classic. Steamboat called it the greatest of his career. The event did do a respectable 4.1 rating on television, but cable companies were so outraged that TBS had cost them pay-per-view buys that Turner executives were chewed out. The WWF had done the same thing to Crockett, killing his promotion, and had been doing the same thing to Turner, but this was apparently less acceptable. With the big show in New Orleans gone, so was JYD. Amazingly, he would return, not once, but twice.

In 1990, WCW called again, with booker Ole Anderson looking for a way to draw black fans back to the sport. Sting had been programmed to replace Ric Flair as the top star of the federation, complete with Flair turning on Sting and reforming the Four Horsemen. Unfortunately, on the night of the big turn, Sting tore up his knee and was out for months. To replace Sting, JYD came in with a huge push as one of the top stars of the federation. To counter the evil Horsemen, the injured Sting put together a group of his own: the Dudes with Attitudes. Along with Sting and JYD, another fading former Mid South star, Paul Orndorff, was enlisted. To say the gimmick failed would be an understatement. Anderson programed JYD to challenge Ric Flair for the WCW title, feeling a run around the Southeast would draw fans seeking the Holy Grail, the "first" black world champion. WCW as a whole was a mess, and Anderson's booking was derided from all sides. Maybe the blame didn't lie with the Junkyard Dog, but his series of title shots didn't draw. The matches were regarded as messes, as well.

Flair, as the saying goes, could have a good match with a broomstick — but even he couldn't get one out of JYD. The two actually headlined the Clash of the Champions XI on June 13, 1990, in Charleston. JYD beat Flair by disqualification when the Horsemen interfered. At the Great American Bash a month later, JYD teamed with Orndorff and El Gigante, a seven-foot former basketball player from Argentina. El Gigante didn't have an ounce of wrestling talent, so naturally he was being pushed as a headliner. The Dudes beat the other three Horsemen by disqualification. In the main event, Sting returned to beat Flair for his much-delayed run on top. Unfortunately, Anderson's booking made a mess of that, as well. The Dog and Flair feud was voted by readers of the *Wrestling Observer* as the worst of the year. Considering that Flair also feuded with Gigante, whose sole notable move was menacing the

JYD and Flair won Pro Wrestling Observer's *"worst feud of the year" in 1990.*

camera and yelling in broken English, "I want da belt," the series with JYD had to be absolutely horrible to earn such an honor.

The Junkyard Dog returned one more time, in 1991, but his time on top was clearly over. He did hold a title during this run; unfortunately, it wasn't one that meant anything. He teamed with Tommy Rich and Ricky Morton to win the WCW six-man championship. They beat Buddy Landel, Dutch Mantel, and Dr. X (probably Jack Victory under a mask), to win the new titles on February 17, 1991, in Atlanta. To show how prestigious they were, the trio defended the titles on the February 24 pay-per-view WrestleWar in Phoenix. They were in the opening match, the curtain jerker as it is called, and beat three glorified jobbers. They would hold the titles until the summer, losing them to the latest and certainly not greatest version of the Freebirds on June 3, 1991, in Birmingham.

In 1992, Watts made the call to the Junkyard Dog — having finally cleared the air after more than seven years of estrangement — to see if he would be able to come back for the Cowboy's version of WCW, but when they met, Watts found JYD in no condition to perform. He wasn't just done with WCW, he was done with the big-time wrestling, period. He lingered on the independent scene, living off his name, making small paydays whenever he could. His reputation grew worse, however, as he continued to miss matches or show up in poor condition. He wrestled in his old haunts across the South, and often received headline status, but he really was used as a mere name from the past. By the late '90s, he was broke and largely out of wrestling.

At one point ECW, the creation of manager-turned-mad-scientist promoter Paul Heyman, honored him at a legends event, but even that was tarnished by an unfortunate incident. ECW star New Jack, alleging that the Junkyard Dog owed him money, caused a huge scene when he attacked JYD outside the ring. It wasn't an angle, just a sad spectacle.

JYD turned 45 in 1998, an age that hadn't prevented Ric Flair, Hulk Hogan, and countless others from headlining huge wrestling shows for major promotions. JYD hadn't been in a main event for seven years. He had been working for an auto repossession company in Mississippi and living with the family that owned the business. According to Meltzer, he had not had a home of his own, or a permanent address, for years.

Several of his friends said Ritter had indicated that he wanted to get off drugs, but he never could. He certainly hadn't turned to the showy, preachy, God-and-wrestling circuit that many of his ex-addict friends and running mates had been working. DiBiase, Landel, Jake Roberts, Tully Blanchard, and many others who had been notorious addicts had all found God and gone clean and sober . . . or, for some, at least found God. DiBiase even used the story of his Mid South best friend as a cautionary tale for his pulpit speeches.

On the June 1, 1998, Sylvester Ritter drove to his hometown of Wadesboro, North Carolina. LaToya, the daughter whose birth he "missed seeing" because of the Freebird angle 18 years earlier, and whose childhood he really did mostly miss because of his career and lifestyle, was graduating from high school. The trip was bitterly disappointing before it turned tragic. Ritter arrived in North Carolina late and missed the graduation. In fact, he missed seeing his daughter entirely — she had left to go to the beach with her friends. Ritter talked to her on the phone, saw and called old friends, and left several days later. When LaToya returned, it was to the news that her father had died.

On the afternoon of June 2, 1998, after spending most of the past 24 hours driving back from North Carolina, Sylvester Ritter fell asleep at the wheel. His car rolled over three times. Ritter broke his neck and was pronounced dead at the scene. LaToya Ritter told the Wadesboro newspaper that her father didn't have a mark on his body. "It was just his time to go," she said.

CHAPTER TEN

A FAN'S TAKE

In June 1984, I was visiting my father in Houston, Texas, as I always did in the summers. My joy at seeing him, my stepsisters, the dog, the swimming pool, my bike, or anything else, paled compared to my joy at catching up on Mid South Wrestling. I had been a wrestling fan for a few months when I discovered Mid South on a visit in 1983, and for the next three years, nothing in Houston was as exciting as returning to find out what was happening on television and what matches were coming to the Sam Houston Coliseum.

I grew up in Maryland, not close enough to the Carolinas to get

Crockett wrestling — although it always surprised me when the Apter magazines mentioned that Mid Atlantic Wrestling was in nearby Virginia — but squarely in prime World Wrestling Federation territory. It isn't that I disliked the WWF. Like a lot of boys growing up, wrestling was one of the few things we all talked about. Even before I started watching, my friends at the bus stop would argue about it. One would show up on a Monday and ask the group, "Did you see what 'Superstar' Billy Graham did to the belt?" Another would reply, "Yes! Can you believe Bob Backlund cried about it?" I had every intention of tuning in to see what they were talking about until the day I saw an ad for the local Capital Centre matches in the sports pages of the *Washington Post*. The ad featured a photo of Andre the Giant, who was so huge, so grotesque, that the very sight of him kept me away from wrestling for several more months. Ultimately, I could not be deterred. In late 1982, while at my grandparents' place in Long Island I came upon a WWF broadcast. The show was almost over when a feature called Buddy Roger's Corner aired. I had no idea who the host was, but he was interviewing a wrestler named Jimmy "Superfly" Snuka. The host told Snuka that his contract with his manager, Lou Albano, was fraudulent, and that Snuka was a free agent. Snuka thanked Rogers, but they both got into an argument with Albano that continued at ringside. There, Snuka was attacked by a pudgy guy named "Crippler" Ray Stevens and piledriven on the concrete several times. Snuka became a bloody mess, and was immobilized and put on a stretcher.

I'm not sure what this said about me, but witnessing this bloody attack got me hooked. It took me on a journey that lasted 15 years, and ended up with me becoming a professional wrestler for a short while. Thirteen years after I left wrestling behind, it led me to write this book. To say my family didn't understand would be an understatement. They encouraged me to watch something else — anything else — but always with no success. My stepfather spent much of the next decade explaining to me that professional wrestling was fake, and he would continue to do so long after I had started reading the newsletters and knew all about the inner workings of the business. Nothing anyone said could stop me from enjoying wrestling. Even girls, who became a preoccupation of mine starting in ninth grade, could only share my attention. Several of my girlfriends and female friends must have been bored to death by my detailed accounts of the latest match or angle. Really, only the boys at the bus stop shared my passion. At least one of my oldest friendships survived the ups and downs of grade school and teen and adult life because of our mutual love of wrestling.

So, when I started to return from my twice-a-year trips to Houston with tapes of Mid South (and, with less attention and fanfare, Texas World Class Championship Wrestling), the guys took notice. We had seen WWF and loved it, but watching Mid South Wrestling was like seeing an R-rated movie after a diet of PG fare. Suddenly, the WWF was no longer as exciting. One of my best friends, a neighbor named Trae, was, and is, a good guy. His dad was the local youth league coach, and Trae was the best athlete in the neighborhood, at least in elementary school. He was the neighborhood guardian, too, a job he worked without distinction. If someone picked on me, he would defend me. If I was picking on someone else, he would defend them against me.

Trae was also black. We lived in a mixed-race neighborhood and went to a mixed-race school in Maryland. It was more than a decade after segregation had ended, and yet we were all conscious of race. You had to be around Trae, because he was very conscious of it. Trae often wanted to play salt-versus-pepper games to prove who was the better athlete, the better boxer, the better wrestler. Most of the time he was on the winning side. I know that Trae's attitude bothered some of the other kids. It never bothered me, although I admit that once or twice I did ask my stepfather to explain why Trae was so fixated on race. He did so in a way that would never leave me, and started me on a journey

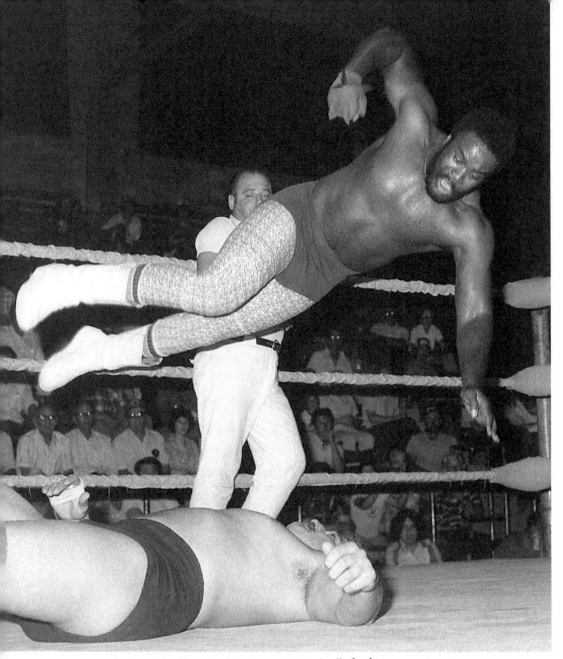

JYD comes in for a hard landing on Jake Roberts, with his deadly fist drop.

of studying race in America, including the civil rights movement, that I continue today.

Trae didn't just like black wrestlers — he loved Bob Backlund, for instance, long after most had determined that he was boring and abandoned him — but he was always interested in the few black wrestlers we knew. Long before I saw him wrestle, I knew of Tony Atlas, and that he had once bested Hulk Hogan. When Rocky Johnson came to the WWF, Trae's joy was unparalleled. Johnson soon became the neighborhood favorite, and my first favorite wrestler, as well. The problem with cheering for Rocky Johnson, as we soon found out, was that his path to the top spot in the federation was blocked.

I remember the chatter at our recreation-league basketball game one Saturday morning after another Roger's Corner in which Buddy Rogers promised to help Rocky Johnson. Johnson told the interviewer that he had been blocked from getting title shots, and that he was in the WWF to win a belt, any belt. He wanted to challenge Bob Backlund for the WWF title; he wanted to challenge Don Muraco for the Intercontinental title; and he wanted to challenge the Samoans for the WWF tag team titles. A week or so later, Rogers came back with some results: Johnson would be granted a title shot against Muraco.

We were excited, but we were also, even as pre-teens, aware that we had witnessed a type of glass ceiling. Johnson never would get a shot at Backlund's world title. He did get a shot at Muraco; the match ended with a screw job. Johnson had the champ in a submission move when Muraco's manager, Albano again, entered the ring. The referee called for the bell. We all thought Johnson had won the title. Instead, Muraco was disqualified for outside interference. Soon enough, they were wrestling at the house shows. We knew a title change must be near, so we begged our parents to take us to the Capital Centre for the next show. Trae's dad took us to the show, but we didn't see a title change, only another disqualification. As far as we knew, Muraco never defeated Johnson, but he didn't lose the belt, either. Soon, Muraco was in a feud with Snuka, instead. Much to Trae's excitement, Tony Atlas returned and teamed with Johnson to win the tag team belts. We rejoiced, but we also knew it wasn't quite the same.

When I returned from Houston with a videotape for the first time, it featured wrestling I knew the other kids had to watch. Trae came over and predictably found a new favorite in the Junkyard Dog. "That brother's the best there is," he marveled. None of us had cable yet, but we had heard about JYD from the magazines; occasionally, we even snuck a peek at him on the Superstation if one of us was visiting a friend or relative with that prized invention. We were surprised at what we saw on Mid South Wrestling. For one thing, the action was much better. Sure, there were some squash matches, but not nearly as many. The WWF formula of five squash matches, an interview, and a main event that was only occasionally of real main-event caliber couldn't compare to the hours of Mid South action. The WWF formula almost never varied. As we grew older, and were exposed to other territories, we grew tired of it. Mid South offered big-name wrestlers facing off against one another all the time. Many weeks, it had two or three big matches on one program. The top wrestlers were always on television (Backlund, for instance, almost never wrestled on television) and the action and angles were so good that even the squash matches were exciting. Often, they didn't even take place as advertised, because they were just a setup for a bigger angle and more excitement. I, for one, was hooked. Mid South became my favorite territory. All these years later, it is still what I consider to be good pro wrestling. I could still sit down with a bunch of Mid South tapes from any of the first six years of the '80s and enjoy them.

Of course, there was the Junkyard Dog, too. As pre-teens, even with Trae's natural hyper-awareness of race, it didn't occur to us that we were seeing something revolutionary. We didn't know that a decision had been made to feature a black man as the star of the territory. We didn't know that there had been protests against this move by some of the local promoters. We didn't know that other wrestling promoters thought Bill Watts was crazy and doomed to failure for his decision. We were living proof of how wrong those promoters were. All of us, white and black, cheered for the Junkyard Dog and loved the promotion that featured him. And this was in 1983, when JYD's weight and drug problems were beginning to hurt his in-ring performances. Everyone looked forward to my trips to Houston and my return with new tapes.

When I say everyone loved the Junkyard Dog, I have to add an honest, ironic caveat. Sometime in 1983, I became a "Hacksaw" Butch Reed fan. It started before I ever saw him wrestle in Mid South. I caught a couple of his matches on the Superstation when he was a babyface feuding with Buzz Sawyer. I devoured magazine articles about him. Soon, I learned about his success in Georgia, and Florida before that. He was a powerhouse with a great physique, and had faster-paced, more exciting matches than JYD. When Reed showed up in Mid South, I cheered. I was thrilled when he beat the crazy Jim Duggan in the battle of the Hacksaws. When Reed shocked everyone by turning on JYD, I turned with him. When Reed won the North American title, it was one of my biggest joys as a wrestling fan. I would remain a Butch Reed fan for many years. I would also begin my half-decade journey into becoming a heel fan, often supporting the bad guys over the good guys, especially when the bad guys were cool or when the good guys were too square, too boring, or got too many squeals from the teenage girls.

This brings me back to 1984. It was spring, and I visited my dad during Easter that school year instead of Christmas. I had arrived just after the Last Stampede and just before JYD left Mid South for good that summer. In reality, although no one could possibly recognize it at that point, Mid South had Duggan, the Junkyard Dog's successor, ready to go. If you only knew Jim Duggan by his late WWF or his entire WCW work you'd miss how big a star he was in Mid South. Almost from the beginning of his tenure under Bill Watts, Duggan had an angel on his shoulder, and a wild mix of enthusiasm and effort. When he turned face, standing up to the hated Arab, Skandar Akbar, when his partner, Ted DiBiase, wanted to sell out to the General, Duggan was immediately a rival to Mr. Wrestling II as the number-two babyface in the territory. By 1984, Duggan's feud with DiBiase had surpassed DiBiase's feud with JYD as the biggest rivalry in the territory, even as it shared time with the ongoing Reed versus JYD saga for top billing. Much like with the Junkyard Dog, Duggan was groomed in a way that kept him away from the top title, the North American belt, for a few years. That left the title firmly revolving around JYD in 1983 (and sort of floating around looking for a top star in 1984 and 1985). While there was no question that JYD was number one and Duggan was number two in the pecking order, the gap was beginning to narrow. Occasionally, Duggan even came in to save the Junkyard Dog when the odds were too great for him, something that was unheard of previously. After all, in the early years the whole JYD gimmick was that he needed no one to save him. He always made his own comeback.

I mention this because in April 1984, while I was watching Mid South Wrestling, I saw perhaps my all-time favorite match. In it, JYD teamed with Duggan to wrestle Reed and his partner/lackey Buddy Landel. As it turned out, the match would set up the final feud of the Junkyard Dog's Mid South career. It was also the kind of action that just didn't take place in the WWF at the time — or at any time — even as it became a bigger deal through its national expansion and began to tinker with its tried-and-true television format, which involved quick squashes.

The match began as many Mid South matches did, with announcer Boyd Pierce — in his weekly game of topping the previous week's outfit with a new one that was even louder — running from the ring as the action began ahead of the bell. In this case, Reed and Landel jumped JYD and Duggan as soon as they entered the ring. As usual in a fair fight, the good guys quickly took over from the heels. Then the match began in earnest. Reed was selling being rocked by the early action, but Landel was doing a job of his own, playing the coward. Repeatedly, he mouthed off to the good guys, encouraged the action, and then attempted to tag out before he could hook up with Duggan. Reed meanwhile, continued to sell, nearly falling on his face. Rather than hook up with Duggan himself, Landel became a cheerleader for Reed, trying to motivate him to get back on his feet and into the ring.

At about the two-minute mark, as Landel was refusing to tag back in the announcers noted that the match now had a new spectator. Jim Cornette and his newly hired bodyguard, Hercules Hernandez, had taken up a position outside the ring, at the bottom of the television screen. Cornette had moved from his Last Stampede feud with Watts and Stagger Lee into a feud with Duggan, going so far as to hire Hernandez to keep "that goofball" away.

At the three-minute mark, the Junkyard Dog finally tagged in. Of course, this was typical of his tag team matches for the length of his run. He immediately put a hurting on Reed, pounding him until he wobbled. Landel finally ran into the ring to make the save, but he got pounded on, too. Within a minute, JYD's work was done, and he tagged back out to Duggan. At this point, the heels finally took over, and the match followed the typical tag team pattern. For nearly two minutes, the heels got heat on Duggan, through both legal and illegal means. Landel played his role, finally accepting a tag once Duggan was down. The two heels pounded Duggan. At that point, JYD entered the ring illegally. "JYD has had enough," Jim Ross boomed, and again the match became a two-on-two brawl.

Next, Cornette, who had been watching relatively quietly, got more animated. "I sure hope he doesn't get involved," Joel Watts said. Of course, it was just seconds before the heel manager did interfere in the match. As Duggan hit the ropes, Cornette pulled the top rope down, leaving Duggan to take a big bump to the concrete. This was done in full view of the referee, causing a disqualification that ended the match. In reality, however, the action was only just beginning.

As Landel and Reed double-teamed JYD in the ring, Cornette put his boots to Duggan. This didn't work very well, so Duggan rose up and attempted to hit Cornette. Hernandez stepped in and leveled Duggan. However, before the bodyguard could press his advantage, JYD's mentor, Sonny King, ran to ringside and knocked Hernandez down with a flying head-butt. Duggan was then able to chase after Cornette. In the bottom corner of the screen, the Midnight Express, Dennis Condrey, and Bobby Eaton appeared to try and stop Duggan. They failed, and got their heads run together instead.

Back in the ring, Landel and Reed took over on JYD. Again, it was a rare time that JYD didn't save himself, although it had to be that way to set up the angle to follow. Duggan cleared the ring with his two-by-four, but before he could celebrate, the heels struck back. Landel tripped Duggan by grabbing his feet, and Duggan lost control of the board. "Ray Hernandez has got the two-by-four," Jim Ross screamed, so excited that he used Hernandez's real first name by mistake. By this point, JYD was on his feet fighting off Reed again, and for some reason he didn't notice what was to come. After a moment of indecision about who to hit, Hernandez settled on Duggan. As he went to strike, however, King threw himself on top of Duggan. Hernandez then brought the weapon down on King's shoulder several times before JYD realized what was going on and cleared the ring with his dog chain.

In the aftermath, of course, JYD and Duggan swore revenge, adding heat to each of their feuds. Mid South banned the use of several foreign objects, including the two-by-four, a tennis racquet, chairs, and a steel chain. Watts often issued various bans on weapons and even specific moves in order to get heat on such offenses and make them seem more dangerous when wrestlers used them. He also used the ban to popularize new weapons. Soon, Duggan and Hernandez would be having coal-miner's-glove matches, with loaded gloves being the new weapon of choice.

In any event, the match is one that I consider a Mid South classic, so good that the lack of a conclusive result didn't matter. Watching it today, I find that it still holds up in terms of action. It is helped tremendously by the crowd, which is really into it. It was also one of the matches that led me to want to become a professional wrestler — but that's another story entirely. It would mark the end of the line, however, for JYD in Mid South. He had about two months left on his legendary journey. Having come to the JYD era very late, and being more of a fan of the era of Duggan, DiBiase, Steve Williams, Terry Taylor, and Butch Reed, it's probably the match that defined JYD's run in Mid South for me.

Of course, for all my love of Mid South, for all my respect (in retrospect) for Sylvester Ritter and his character, I was not his main target audience. I was in Houston, not New Orleans. When I did get to go to matches a year or two later, they were at the Sam Houston Coliseum and not the Superdome or the Municipal Auditorium. I did not witness firsthand, or in some cases even later on tape, most of the classic angles that defined JYD's run. And, it pains me to admit, I was not a black fan overjoyed at the prospect of seeing a wrestler of my skin color portrayed as the best of the best. This all led me to want to know more about the love affair that Mid South, and in particular New Orleans, had with the Junkyard Dog from 1979–1984. Once I learned the whole story, it led me to want to do something more for the memory of Sylvester Ritter.

A FORGOTTEN HERO

As is the case with most professional wrestlers, Sylvester Ritter's death did not get much media coverage, at least not in the mainstream media. Hey, it's just fake wrestling, right? Wrestling deaths don't matter. The only exception is when the deaths are tabloid fodder — murder-suicides or tragic falls from spectacular heights. Occasionally, the number of deaths from drugs, especially cocaine and performance-enhancing drugs, pile up. Then someone writes an exposé with a huge list of names of wrestlers who have died young. Individual deaths are rarely treated as celebrity deaths. Features, like career retrospectives, are rarely commissioned, even for the most famous wrestlers. Quite often, even basic obituaries are hard to find, except those of longtime regional stars who stayed in one territory for most of their careers. Sometimes you can also find wrestlers' obituaries in their hometown papers.

So it was for the professional wrestler known as the Junkyard Dog. The New Orleans newspaper, *The Times-Picayune,* missed the story completely. The paper's writers and editors were either unaware of or uninterested in the death of a professional wrestler, even one that had been a bigger star in New Orleans than Archie Manning or Pete Maravich. The wrestling community noted JYD's death, to be sure, especially in publications like the *Wrestling Observer*, which has become a sort of history book of the sport's otherwise forgotten stories. However, the only wrestler or wrestling official to attend the funeral was Buddy Landel. Landel, who has apparently beaten his own awful drug issues and has now become a lay minister, has a tribute to JYD posted on his web site. It is free-verse poetry that is filled with sorrow for a lost friend. Several thousand citizens of the town of Wadesboro did turn out to say goodbye to their local star. Watts, DiBiase, the Funks, the McMahons, and others sent flowers or condolences. So, reportedly, did a much bigger North Carolina hero and legend, Michael Jordan.

When wrestlers began dying young like it was an epidemic, no one covered the story with more fact-based, grammatically awkward, melancholy obituaries than Dave Meltzer. Meltzer's obituaries were and are an Irish wake and a history lesson — or a semester — jammed into an eight- to 20-page newsletter. As the person who chronicled these deaths, Meltzer described the phenomenon in wrestling known as the call. It comes from a friend, someone you haven't heard from in a while — only it comes at 3 a.m. and they are rambling or they have been drinking. When you answer the phone, they start talking, sometimes at length, before they spill the news, but you know right away that someone has died.

In 1998, "the call" went out about Sylvester Ritter. Unlike many other wrestling deaths, however, there was no 10-bell salute, no rushed tribute on the Monday-night cable shows. The Junkyard Dog was mentioned in passing, and then it was on to the angle of the moment. Of course, Ritter did have an unusual death for the era. While drugs ruined his career, there is no indication that they caused his death. Instead, he died a more traditional wrestling death — a victim of the road. His WWF foe, Adrian Adonis, died in a similar fashion in Canada. And way back when JYD was becoming the king of New Orleans, Tri-State had lost its big star when Danny Hodge suffered career-ending injuries in a car wreck.

Still, dying in a car wreck is no better than an overdose or a suicide in wrestling or any other walk of life. Whatever the details, Sylvester Ritter was gone, and after wrestling and the world at large had moved on, many of his friends had not. Many indicated their hopes for him to kick his addictions, or for a never-realized comeback. Others saluted his never-ending generosity, and how, even when he was down and out, he would always help someone in need.

In very few arenas or publications, however, was Sylvester Ritter remembered for being a groundbreaking athlete, a premium draw, or a history-making wrestler. Furthermore, in very few places in his old stomping grounds, in the Dog's Yard, so to speak, was he remembered at all. Sadly, this trend continues and gets worse as the years pass.

As the NFL's Saints marched to the Superbowl in 2010, the chants of "Who Dat?" and "Who Dat Think They Gunna Beat Dem Saints?" filled the 'Dome and caused much reflection on the phrase's roots. *The Times-Picayune* even ran a front-page article on the subject, complete with a full-page-long jump that ran down the history of the phrase from music to black culture to high school football to the Saints. The article never mentioned the Junkyard Dog. *The Times-Picayune*, which missed the obituary, also missed that piece of "Who Dat?" history. In the paper's defense, the legends surrounding the chant are complex and claims to it are never ending. The newspaper's reporter, Dave Walker, did not want to be quoted on the subject; however, he did indicate that since the story ran he has been overwhelmed by people claiming that they were the ones who started the chant.

Sylvester Ritter is better remembered on the historical circuit. At first glance, it might not seem like much, but a small movement has developed around the history of wrestling. There are now three viable halls of fame for wrestlers, the *Wrestling Observer* Hall of Fame, the WWE Hall of Fame, and the Pro Wrestling Hall of Fame. The latter is an actual museum in the upstate New York city of Amsterdam. In addition, there are many venues with their own halls of fame, and some of them feature wrestlers. For instance, the Madison Square Garden in New York City has a walk of fame whose inductees include Hulk Hogan, Bruno Sammartino, Bob Backlund, and other wrestlers and wrestling personnel from the WWF, WWWF, and WWE eras.

The most clear-cut and unfortunate omission is actually the most logical. Dave Meltzer's *Wrestling Observer Newsletter* offers the most clearly reasoned rules for a wrestling hall of fame. Meltzer set up the newsletter's hall of fame with a model of the National Baseball Hall of Fame in Cooperstown, New York. Every year, a mix of active and retired wrestlers and wrestling officials, wrestling journalists and experts vote in a new class of legends. The *Wrestling Observer Newsletter* Hall of Fame has set criteria for judging worthiness. Because it is wrestling, no actual standard of wins and losses applies. The criteria are based on four areas: length of time as a headline attraction, historic significance, ability to attract viewers, and wrestling ability. Clearly, for the Junkyard Dog, the criteria splits votes. In Mid South, he had a great ability to attract viewers, although the territory did as well or better for a few more years after he left. Historical significance is unquestionably JYD's greatest claim to fame. He was a pioneer with regard to race and wrestling, and the wrestler who made a city and territory significant to the sport.

There have clearly been few wrestlers who have drawn more fans to a city over a five-year period than the Junkyard Dog did in New Orleans. Meltzer and his sources may be able to come up with a list of wrestlers who drew better in one city over a period of time, but I can't think of anyone. For the Junkyard Dog, the question then became, in the eyes of *Wrestling Observer Newsletter* Hall of Fame voters, was that enough? Their answer was no. Clearly, JYD had deficits. Mainly, he was never a hall-of-fame worker in terms of wrestling ability. Also, as much as anything else, longevity was a problem. His Mid South reign lasted just under five years. The run in the WWF lasted less than that and was not, except for a short time at the beginning, of main-event caliber. Compared to acts like Ric Flair, Dusty Rhodes, and Hulk Hogan, who were on top for decades, the Junkyard Dog was a shooting star. The panel did not vote JYD into the *Wrestling Observer Newsletter* Hall of Fame, and he has been dropped from the ballot. In theory, he could return, but so far there has been no enthusiasm for his inclusion in the *Observer*'s hall of fame.

The Pro Wrestling Hall of Fame in upstate New York also did not include the Junkyard Dog, until recently. The hall has space limitations, and it seems to be more about inducting a select few wrestlers every year than following the *Wrestling Observer Newsletter* approach, which consisted of a wave of early inductees followed by newly eligible candidates competing with guys who got enough votes to stay on the ballot. The Pro Wrestling Hall of Fame has not inducted as many members as the *Wrestling Observer Newsletter* Hall of Fame, and is running behind the others in inducting certain members. Ted DiBiase, for instance, was just inducted in 2008, and Bobo Brazil had to wait until 2009. As this book was going to press, it was announced that JYD will be immortalized at the Pro Wrestling Hall of Fame, inducted in May with their 2012 class.

The other wrestling hall to induct the Junkyard Dog has the least objective standards, the WWE Hall of Fame. This hall of fame is widely regarded as less of a reflection of the history of professional wrestling than as a reflection of the history of professional wrestling when viewed through the filter or the bias of the WWWF, the WWF, and WWE. While many of the inductees, perhaps even most of them, are legitimate hall of famers — Ernie Ladd and Bobo Brazil, to use just two examples, are in all three halls of fame — there are certainly people who have been good employees, politically connected, or favorites within the WWE rather than bona fide hall of famers. Included in the list are two wrestlers, Johnny Rodz and "Baron" Mikel Scicluna, who were mostly used as job guys. When the WWE reached a deal with the sole surviving Von Erich brother, Kevin, to buy the WCCW tape collection, it inducted the Von Erich family into its hall of fame. Fritz, David, Kerry, and Kevin were all main-event talent, and a case can be made for any of them to be in a hall of fame. although a case could also be made against them, too. However, the WWE inducted Chris and Mike Von Erich, as well. Neither brother was very good in the ring; Mike was awful, and Chris was too small to enjoy more than a few gimmick matches with managers. Both wound up committing suicide — their lone contribution to the history of wrestling was as part of a family history of tragedy. That same year, the WWE Hall of Fame inducted Howard Finkle, a longtime ring announcer. In addition, the hall has inducted several celebrity novelty acts who have appeared at special events, mostly WrestleManias; these acts include announcer Bob Uecker, NFL player William "the Refrigerator" Perry, and baseball outcast Pete Rose; the latter took all sorts of scripted abuse in WWE rings, and was inducted to spite Major League Baseball, which still has not allowed Rose to be considered for induction into the National Baseball Hall of Fame. The list of questionable inductees is very long, and perhaps it waters down the inclusion of the Junkyard Dog.

The fact remains that of the three halls of fame, it was the WWE Hall of Fame that was first to induct JYD. The induction took place in 2004. Ladd inducted JYD posthumously, and Latoya Ritter accepted the award for her father. JYD's inclusion should not be questioned. He had enough of a run at a crucial time for the WWF. He certainly was an important figure in wrestling overall. He was bigger in the WWF than any of the previously mentioned names, or for that matter than Koko B. Ware, a mid-card face who replaced JYD on the follow-up to *The Wrestling Album*, but could never fill his boots in the ring. Ware, too, is in the WWE Hall of Fame. His song, "Piledriver," and his Blue Macaw, Frankie, far outshone his in-ring work or historical significance.

In addition, many wrestlers have been inducted for their work outside of McMahon-promoted wrestling. Verne Gagne, Bill Watts, the Von Erichs, the Blackjacks, and many others, including Brazil and Ladd, had accomplishments that were largely made in other promotions, indeed, sometimes in their own promotions. Of the Von Erichs, only Kerry Von Erich had a WWF run, and that wouldn't merit inclusion on its own.

On the local level, more hope can be found in the state halls of fame. Currently, Sylvester Ritter has not been inducted into any sports halls of fame. However, there is an interest in his accomplishments. The Louisiana Sports Hall of Fame in Natchitoches, Louisiana, has inducted Ernie Ladd. Ladd, of course, had a football background that helped. For Ritter, the case is less clear. His high school and college accomplishments were in North Carolina, not Louisiana. However, during the process of researching the possible ways of honoring JYD, the Louisiana Sports Hall of Fame has agreed to present JYD for possible membership.

"As it stands today," said director Doug Ireland, "I'd just guess that he would be viewed like a D. Wayne Lucas would be in horse racing if he had great success at Louisiana tracks. It's a very interesting situation. No doubt, he was very popular and had great success here. Let's see how it plays out . . ." Ireland said the issue of pro wrestling has not been addressed, but he encouraged a submission of the Junkyard Dog's name.

In response, I submitted the following description of JYD for his induction application: "Sylvester Ritter, better known as the Junkyard Dog, 1952–1998, was the star of Mid South Wrestling from 1979–1984. He was the first African-American wrestler to be made the top star of an entire wrestling territory, a feat more remarkable given the history of racial unrest in the Deep South, as well as the backlash during the civil rights era. Louisiana's system of sanctioning wrestling required local political appointees to serve as promoters for Mid South Wrestling, and in many instances, they objected to Ritter being booked as the star of the show. Despite this, Mid South had great success with its star, and became one of the top promotions in the country during his run. The heart of MSW was the state of Louisiana, where Mid South taped television matches in Shreveport and ran weekly events at the Downtown Municipal Auditorium in New Orleans, as well as three to five Superdome Spectaculars a year. Ritter, who lived in Baton Rouge during this era, set a record in 1980 for an indoor wrestling event, drawing more than 26,000 fans to the 'Dome for his main event against Michael Hayes of the Fabulous Freebirds. Over the course of his run, he probably drew more than one million fans to New Orleans for wrestling events. The Municipal Auditorium, where an average of 5,000 fans per week went to see the shows, gained the nickname 'the Dog's Yard,' and it is believed that JYD never lost a match there until 1984. During his run, the fans were known to chant, 'who dat think they gunna beat that dog?' Although the chant did not originate with JYD, it is possible that it transferred from him to the Saints, as the chant first began to be used for the Saints in 1983, in the middle of his run. In the ring, Ritter held every title in Mid South, including the North American Heavyweight Championship. He had many memorable feuds, most notably with Ted DiBiase, Butch Reed, Paul Orndorff, 'Mr. Olympia' Jerry Stubbs, the Fabulous Freebirds, and the 'Big Cat' Ernie Ladd. In 1984, Ritter left Mid South for the World Wrestling Federation, where he was a top star for the rest of the decade. He died in 1998 in a car accident in Forest, Mississippi. His accomplishments have largely been forgotten in the city and state where he was once a huge star." In his first attempt, Ritter was not voted into the 2011 class of Louisiana Sports Hall of Fame, which was a New Orleans Saints–heavy induction class. However, there is hope that he will be in a future class.

The experience and information I gained in the submission process helped me realize that North Carolina might be another place to honor Ritter. Much like the Louisiana version, the North Carolina Sports Hall of Fame, in Raleigh, North Carolina, places an emphasis on native sons and daughters. Its requirements for non-natives is a bit more clear, although in the case of JYD it doesn't matter, since he was born, raised, and played sports in North Carolina. There are no wrestlers currently in the North Carolina Sports Hall of Fame, and considering that Richard Flier, a.k.a. Ric Flair, is a longtime Charlotte resident, that probably isn't a good sign. However, Earl "Curly" Neal is in the hall, and while he was a high school basketball star in North Carolina, his main success is as a member of the Harlem Globetrotters, who play a sport that, like pro wrestling, is fixed. Neal's case may also provide a lifeline, however, as his induction is based in large part on his North Carolina roots. As he would later exaggerate with the Globetrotters, Neal was a dribbling freak of nature, a legend that extends down to his developing days. Along with the fact that Sylvester Ritter grew up in North Carolina, his high school and college football experience and his modest success in high school wrestling and track and field might also be enough to put him over the top as an inductee. It wouldn't be an honor to him as a wrestler or as a pioneer in post–civil rights achievement, but it would be an honor for Sylvester Ritter the man. Recently, I submitted Sylvester Ritter for North Carolina Sports Hall of Fame membership, as well.

Ritter could also be recognized for his civic contribution. There are several options in New Orleans and the region in general. The Superdome could decide to have its own hall of fame, or walk of fame. Both options are made more likely by the Saints' 2010 Super Bowl win, the first in the franchise's long history of losing. In addition, the Downtown Municipal Auditorium, although it is still damaged and vacant in the wake of Hurricane Katrina, is part of a larger rebuilding effort in the neighborhood of Treme. The cultural center next to the Auditorium, the Mahalia Jackson Center, has been renovated and hosts plays, musicals, and all sorts of community events. Around the two buildings is a wider complex, the Louis Armstrong Park. The park is still under construction, but it is expected that it will honor many cultural heroes of New Orleans. It is still possible that a sculpture or plaque honoring Sylvester Ritter could be added to the area. In some respect, even more than the Superdome, the grounds outside the auditorium are probably exactly where a monument to JYD should be.

It would be a shame if the Junkyard Dog went down to defeat at the hands of indifference, forgotten memories, or a lack of financial or political clout. However, I don't expect that will happen. I believe that readers of this book will help contribute to honoring his memory. Sylvester Ritter's legacy as the Junkyard Dog is one story that has only just begun.

At ECW Press, we want you to enjoy this book in whatever format you like, whenever you like. Leave your print book at home and take the eBook to go! Purchase the print edition and receive the eBook free. Just send an email to ebook@ecwpress.com and include:

- the book title
- the name of the store where you purchased it
- your receipt number
- your preference of file type: PDF or ePub?

A real person will respond to your email with your eBook attached. And thanks for supporting an independently owned publisher with your purchase!